Independent
London
store guide

D1009747

In memory of photographer Ursula Steiger

Moritz Steiger and Effie Fotaki
MONSTERMEDIA PUBLISHING

Salutations Independent London shoppers!

It's been a turbulent year with the international financial gambling community bringing us all a cropper. No doubt their bonuses are still guaranteed. Out of interest when is a bonus 'not a bonus'?

With two huge new global brand shopping developments either side of the city, in Shepherds Bush and Stratford; as well as tough times for the average shopper and shop vacancies at an all time high, life has been difficult for independent shops in London.

In east London what looks like a shoe-in for big brands, is another missed opportunity, the Bishopsgate Goods Yard Boxpark temporary retail development. Seemingly geared towards big brands looking for some Shoreditch-street-cred, could this be the end to the Shoreditch we know and love if the big brands make the site their own?

It's vital we keep these corporate developments in check and try to preserve our high streets where true communities exist.

Nonetheless we have forged on with a new edition of our book because the signs are good. Plenty of enterprise and new endeavour, especially in the east end where there have been plenty of new shops opening. Vintage and Crafts show no sign of abating. We have tried to include all types of independent traders whether they are pub owners, butchers or artists.

★ **Look out for the in-shop offers with this book.**
Some discounts may be available for a limited period and only on selected items.

Contents

East London is both the capital's self-styled epicenter of cool and home to diverse multicultural communities. For hip-hunters, it's the ultimate place for staying on the pulse, be it the arts (The White Cube on Hoxton Square) or the latest fashion trends – you need only walk around the vintage markets bursting out of Brick Lane and Spitalfields. Raging nightlife makes it a hotspot after dark too with Shoreditch's clubs and bars providing something for everyone, from sound system raving at indie den XOYO to artsy events and exhibitions at clued-up café-cum-bar The Book Club. Just make sure you stop off at one of the many Vietnamese restaurants along Kingsland Road before you head out – Song Que is our clear favourite.

N1 *Hoxton*

E2/EC2 *Shoreditch*

E1 *Spitalfields*

E1 *Brick Lane*

E2 *Columbia Road*

E8 *Dalston*

E8 *Broadway Market*

E1 *London Field's*

E9 *Well Street*

E5 *Chatsworth Road*

E9 *Hackney Wick*

E9 *Victoria Village*

EAST

BookArtBookshop is a place for those with an obsessive love of words and paper. A unique shop that sells handmade, limited edition books made by artists and small press publishers such as Red Fox and Concrete Hermit, its range includes obscure publications on arcane subjects ranging from pataphysics to surrealism. Here you will find books of all shapes and sizes, some screen-printed, some hand-typed, some with covers made of perspex or bubble wrap and some where you won't know if it's a book or a sculpture. It's a perfect starting point for any budding illustrator to find inspiration. In addition to hosting lectures, discussions and book launches, owner Tanya wanted to devise a space to support others using the window display as an opportunity for local artists and students to show their works as well as lovingly displaying a wide range of their books and hand-printed cards and postcards. *PB*

MAP 3 Ref. 40
BookArtBookshop
17 Pitfield Street
Hoxton N1 6HB
+44 (0)20 7608 1333
www.bookartbookshop.com
Wed–Fri 1–7pm
Sat 12–6pm

Don't invite these guys into your house. Furniture in the current range by this collective features just about anything deemed surplus to requirements. Generally that means stuff they've scavenged, things people leave for them outside the shop and redundant materials that the council can't shift. But the latest iteration of their Coffee Kart bears a grab rail foraged from their own bathroom. Surplus you see. If they had a mission statement, it might suggest their intention is to gobble up all our waste and spit it out more useful, in an effort to teach us something. But at the moment, they're probably too busy teaching their Italian graphic designer to spell, before their brochures go off the scale from enchantingly dyslexic to plain surreal. Life moves pretty fast for **East London Furniture**. If you don't stop by Hoxton Street quite soon you might miss them. See website for location details. *GT*

MAP 3 Ref. 48

East London Furniture
151 Hoxton Street
Hoxton N1 6PJ
+44 (0)7522 967 269
www.eastlondonfurniture.co.uk
Mon–Fri 11–7pm
Sat 11–6.30pm
New address from end of March:
46 Willow Walk SE1 5SF

Discount*

This menswear store located on a cobbled street off Hoxton Square is where you would come to find high end Japanese streetwear brands. Here they can tell you why only the Japanese can make jeans the way they should be made and why you should settle for nothing less than a 'salvaged edge' made on an old fashioned loom (much harder wearing apparently). **Goodhood** stocks a range of independent streetwear designers from all over the world who only do limited runs so you are unlikely to ever find someone wearing the same piece. Matt black walls, t-shirts hung with equal spacing and a glass floor where you can spy on their design studio downstairs make Goodhood feel a bit like an art gallery. Their range of trendy magazines, solid silver jewellery with swan heads and skulls with Minnie Mouse ears make this store the epitome of Hoxton-cool. *PB*

MAP 3 Ref. 39

Goodhood

41 Coronet Street

Hoxton N1 6HD

+44 (0)20 7729 3600

www.goodhoodstore.co.uk

Mon–Fri 11–7pm

Sat 11–6.30pm

Operated by the Ministry of Stories, an organisation run by volunteers that holds writing workshops for local children, **Monster Supplies** was formed, an old-fashioned store front selling 'sweets' and other gifts for monsters. "Tins of Fear", horror stories written by ten year olds sit on a shelf titled Mortal Terror underneath the bottles of bile and finger nail clippings. The first question you'll be asked when you walk in is if you are looking for a gift for any particular kind of monster, in which case you'll be directed to either Zombie Mints (for Zombies with bad breath) or 'Thickest Snot' and 'Cubed Earwax', (sure favourites of any monster). Along with the invisible cat and shelf with a monster sized bite taken out of it, the façade never ends. *PB*

MAP 3 Ref. 49

Hoxton Street Monster supplies
159 Hoxton Street
Hoxton N1 6PJ
+44 (0)20 7729 4159
www.monstersupplies.org
Tue – Fri
1pm – 5pm
Sat 11am – 5pm

On one of London's more authentic East End streets, a stone's throw from Shoreditch and nestled between a chicken shop and a newsagents, is the most stylish florist-cum-café you will ever hope to find. With a background of 10 years working with the likes of Alexander McQueen and Christian Louboutin, **The Willow Shoreditch** owner, Ying, knows what 'chic' should look like. The shop is divided into two halves, "flowers at the front, food at the back and things in between". All the food, the delicious salads and cakes are made fresh that morning by Ying himself. It may have been done on a shoe string, but the elegant interior, comprised of reclaimed wood and quirky furniture, with a constantly changing theme to co-ordinate with the flowers is evidence that some people just have a true knack of making something out of nothing. *PB*

MAP 3 Ref. 47

The Willow Shoreditch

92 Hoxton Street

Hoxton N1 6LP

+44 (0)20 7739 3009

www.thewillowshoreditch.com

Mon–Fri 10.30–5pm

Sat 11–4pm

A clothes boutique for the super-chic who chant the mantra "black never goes out of style". Here they have a neatly edited selection of pieces with emphasis on black, studs, leather, sequins and glass beads. **11 Boundary** is a nod to those that know their look and like to add to their ever expanding wardrobe of black and studs. You will find sleek garments in muted tones and soft fabrics by the likes of Twenty8Twelve, L.A.M.B and C'N'C Costume National. There is a good selection of shoes from Vivienne Westwood + Melissa and Sam Edelman and delicate jewellery by the likes of House of Harlow. The look of the steely fashion editor wouldn't be complete however without a pair of sunglasses by Tom Ford. *PB*

MAP 2 Ref. 29
11 Boundary
11 Boundary Street
Shoreditch E2 7JE
+44 (0)20 7033 0310
www.11boundary.com
Tue–Sat 10–7pm
Thu 10–8pm
Sun 11–5pm

3939 cleverly borrows the Japanese words for the number three (which is 'san') and nine ('kyu') to come up with its store name: 'thank you thank you'. Inside, the edit of lesser-known clothing labels and accessories is just as imaginative, with eccentric, colourful apparel by brands including Swash and Sibling among striking jewellery by labels such as Dogstate, as well as distinctive shoes and bags by the likes of Mors, Ki:ts and Jas MB. It's not all fashion though: the boutique also operates as a selling gallery, exhibiting work by contemporary artists and photographers. Previous exhibitions have showcased the talents of Beatrice Boyle, Damien Poulain and Mari Sarai, while a host of other creatives can be discovered among a select cut of art books and cult magazines. ZA

MAP 2 Ref. 41

3939 Shop

8 Kingsland Road

Shoreditch E2 8DA

+44 (0)20 7033 0352

www.3939shop.com

Tue–Sun 12pm– 7pm

It all started 30 years ago when a young punk from Yorkshire went to London in search of kindred spirits, only to find what he was looking for at World's End, the renowned shop owned by Malcolm McLaren and Vivienne Westwood. It was here he met their son Joe and a long lasting friendship was born. **A Child of the Jago**, aptly named after the 1896 novel depicting the violence and crime the area was prone to, came about, well, out of thin air really. With an interior like the inside of a pirate's ship or a circus tent, it doesn't have the feel of a standard shop, more of a museum where everything is for sale. Upstairs you will find hand tailored pieces made within walking distance of the shop and downstairs a collection of beautiful antique clothing, from late 1800's French cavalry jackets to Chinese circus outfits and 1940's hunting breeches. *PB*

MAP 2 Ref. 31

A Child of the Jago
10 Great Eastern Street
Shoreditch EC2A 3NT
+44 (0)20 7377 8694
www.achildofthejago.com
Mon–Sat 11–7pm
Sun 12–5pm

Shoreditch. *Fashion*

15

East End's **Anthem** provides the fashionable gent with a filtered shopping experience, a sort of capsule edit of the best men's labels. Co-founded by Liberty's former head of menswear, Simon Spiteri, the selection is as refined as you would expect. Brands such as Folk, Oliver Spencer, Larke and Rag & Bone hang beside less familiar international labels such as Paris's Yves Andrieux and Norway's Nanok – and the result is a varied and enticing mix of apparel in complete contrast to the high street's throwaway fast-fashion. Spiteri and his business partner Jeremy Baron travel the world sourcing not only interesting men's garb, but also odd bits of beautiful furniture and accessories to decorate the store. You'll likely spot different pieces every time you visit as the items they bring back (think gorgeous antique filing cabinets and hand-felted Persian rugs) are price-tagged and sold on. ZA

MAP 2 Ref. 35

Anthem

10–12 Calvert Avenue

Shoreditch E2 7JP

+44 (0)207 033 0054

www.anthemstore.co.uk

Mon–Fri 11–7pm

Sat 11–6.30pm

Sun 12–5pm

Now if we're talking interiors then **The Bridge Coffee House** is totally unparalleled. This is one hell of a collection of stuff, seamlessly traversing across many time periods and continents. Fuchsia pink upholstered chairs mixed with framed photographs of Robert de Niro and Wild West heroes, vintage fluorescent signs, chandeliers, Tiffany lamps and exotic furniture make this the most visually exciting café I have ever seen. The owner Ricco has designed every inch himself from the door handles to the priceless collection itself, "If I see something I like and I can afford it, I buy it, I don't wait for tomorrow, you have to have a passion". Well The Bridge certainly has passion. The delicious coffee and selection of over-the-top creamy cakes make this the perfect spot to while away the time, although don't go if keeping eye contact is required, it's all just too distracting. *PB*

MAP 3 Ref. 44

The Bridge Coffee House
15 Kingsland Road
Shoreditch E2 8AA
+44 (0)20 3489 2216
Mon–Wed 8–1am
Thu–Sat 8–2am
Sun 10–12am

Shoreditch . **Cafe**

On a stretch of land, pretty much solely inhabited by Vietnamese restaurants, was launched **The Grocery** because as the owner puts it, 'there was nowhere to buy food round here'. Here they make doing your weekly food shop fun. You feel healthy just setting foot in the place. The exposed brick walls and shelves stacked with 12 different types of organic sugar, remind you how much fun cooking can be. Although it may be misconstrued as somewhat pretentious, they don't care.

For healthy types there is nothing you won't find here, from every different kind of gluten free flour to organic vegetables. They even stock an extensive range of hair and beauty products whereby you will never go to Boots again. Now if the deli section wasn't satisfying enough there is a café tucked away at the back with big country kitchen style wooden tables and copies of The Guardian strewn about, serving the best coffee and delicious food from homemade soup to quiche and fancy scrambled eggs. *PB*

MAP 3 Ref. 46
The Grocery
54-58 Kingsland Road
Shoreditch E2 8DP
+44 (0)20 7729 6855
www.thegroceryshop.co.uk
Mon–Sun 8–10pm

Black Hessian lines the walls of this sartorial boutique mixing eclectic and modern menswear with "Goth Drapery", avant-garde clothes with impeccable style, quality and finish in varying shades of black. The elegant, worn aesthetic of the store houses streetwear inspired brands for those that 10 years ago wore Stussy but are now more inclined to wear Adam Kimmel or Mastermind Japan. Semi-bespoke beautifully tailored pieces from the likes of Rik Owens, Damir Doma and Ann Demeulemeester and rails of black jumpers in various different cuts, shades and fabrics complete the store's 'grown-up concept'. With previous experience running the Dover Street Market, **Hostem** is run by men who know and love fashion and the pieces come at a price which reflects the product and the attention to detail. *PB*

MAP 2 Ref. 27
Hostem
41–43 Redchurch Street
Shoreditch E2 7DJ
+44 (0)20 7739 9733
www.hostem.co.uk
Tue–Sat 11–7pm
Sun 12–5pm

Shoreditch . *Fashion*

Buying the most boring household items has never been so fun. **Labour and Wait** specialise in timeless homewares, traditional and simple, right down to the enamel lampshades and unbleached cotton oven gloves. Purchasing a dustpan and brush has taken on a whole new slant! Tired of buying cheap disposable items destined for the garbage after only a few uses, the owners decided to compile and sell everything you need for your home – useful things that will last, probably outlasting you. With a cool calm atmosphere and shelves stacked with an art gallery aesthetic, from enamel coffee pots and bread tins to horsehair brooms, linen dishtowels and old-fashioned school notebooks you can come back time and again, safe in the knowledge that you will always find what you saw last time you were there. *PB*

MAP 2 Ref. 25

Labour and Wait

85 Redchurch Street

Shoreditch E2 7DJ

+44 (0)20 7729 6253

www.labourandwait.co.uk

Tue–Sun 11–6pm

So you need a few basic items, some door hooks, a clock, a few plates or a birthday present perhaps? Well **Lifestyle Bazaar** will sort you out, here you will find a product designer's playground, it's like a mini museum of ideas, how to take the utilitarian and make it an art piece. Don't be intimated by the recycled paper clocks, or the wonders that can be made out of ceramic and glass as it may look expensive but is in fact very affordable. The owners understand that interior design shops can be alienating but here they have a whole wealth of things that you never knew you couldn't live without. Like a designer homeware version of an Italian Deli piled high with exotic food but in their case glass vase fridge magnets, designer chopping boards and Japanese style lunch boxes. *PB*

MAP 3 Ref. 42
Lifestyle Bazaar
11a Kingsland Road
Shoreditch E2 8AA
+44 (0)20 7739 9427
www.lifestylebazaar.com
Tue–Sat 11–7pm
Sun 12–5pm

Luna & Curious

Set up by a group who wanted a space to showcase their work, **Luna & Curious** now sell products from many designers ranging from fashion and jewellery to tea sets and gift cards, the only brief being that the product has a story behind it. Most of the things in the shop take a simple theme and add a whimsical flourish, such as delicate white mugs, plates and tea pots with protruding ceramic butterflies or elegant candle sticks made out of drainpipes. The theme is inspired by "weird ideas you get when you wake up in the middle of the night". It's the way things are displayed on tables and chairs cut in half and mounted on the wall that make it nearly as much an art gallery as a shop. *PB*

MAP 2 Ref. 24
Luna & Curious
24 – 26 Calvert Avenue
Shoreditch E2 7JP
+44 (0)20 3222 0034
www.lunaandcurious.com
Mon–Sun 11–6pm

With a long history in museum retail, owner Noah has created a design gift shop that doesn't take itself too seriously. At **Maiden** you will find witty cards and fridge magnets stacked on top of an old 60's ironing board and pulp fiction novels piled high on an iron garden bench. There isn't a particular theme as such, just random stuff you don't need but really really want, be it a mask of Charlie Chaplin or a book on Yves Saint Laurent – he just wants you to laugh your way around the shop. Noah likes to think of it as an Aladdin's cave where he is Aladdin and does everything from choose what he sells to sweeping the floor. "I like to walk into a shop and see things that I can afford" he says, so you won't have a problem finding a gift as price tags range from anywhere between 80p to £200. *PB*

MAP 2 Ref. 30
Maiden
188 Shoreditch High Street
Shoreditch E1 6HU
+44 (0)20 7998 0185
www.maidenshop.com
Mon–Sat 11–7pm

-10%
Discount*

Milk

In a unique eighteenth century building on Shoreditch's main thoroughfare is **Milk**, a 'concept boutique' owned by a couple who love to travel, a fact reflected in their eclectic taste and choice of international designers. They call it a concept boutique because each brand has a concept behind it, whether it's perfume from Laura Tonatto, described in Italy as the most highly esteemed Italian nose having created innovative fragrances for 20 years, or shoes by Repetto one of the oldest makers of ballet shoes in the world. A brilliant collection of quirky modern designs most notably by Fornasetti the Italian sculptor whose trademark is the distinctive motif of operetta soprano Lina Cavalieri's face printed on everything from porcelain plates to cushions. They sell pieces they love, focusing on small furniture items catering for the small spaces people inhabit in London, including inspired handcrafted lighting, whimsical coffee tables and umbrella stands. *PB*

MAP 2 Ref. 38

Milk
118½ Shoreditch High Street
Shoreditch E1 6JN
+44 (0)20 7729 9880
www.milkconceptboutique.eu
Mon–Fri 11–7pm
Thu 11–8pm
Sat 11–6pm
Sun 10.30–6pm

-10%

*Discount on fashion items only**

You have to find it first, an obscure door marked **MJM** will lead you up a steep staircase plastered with strange graphic images to a bright showroom of designs by Hong Kong born Makin Jan Ma, a fashion designer with an unusual approach to fashion. Originally wanting to make films he would design outfits for his characters, fast forward he is now a sought after cult label in Japan, with a strong following worldwide and stockists including Top Shop. The showroom itself is in the same building he lives and shares with a group of other creative people. What used to be their kitchen is now the MJM showroom displaying pieces of great quality using unusual fabrics and bright prints, it just goes to show what great things can easily be missed. *PB*

MAP 3 Ref. 45

MJM store
17A Kingsland Road
Shoreditch E2 8AA
+44 (0)20 7739 3699
www.mjm-store.com
www.makinjanma.com
Wed–Sun 3pm–8pm

-15%

Discount*

Nobrow was created by a couple of illustrators with a love of comics and graphic novels who wanted to publish their own work and the work of artists they love. With their design studios in the back and a gallery downstairs, the shop provides a showcase for the graphic books and magazines they publish, alongside the works of other publishers they admire. With around 35 publications spanning from graphic novels to children's books, their magazine 'Nobrow' is their flagship product. Giving artists a double page spread to be freely creative and by using a different printing process which gives it a distinctive aesthetic makes each issue a collectable. The concept of the shop comes down to a strong reaction against the death of print and a continuing love for printed books. *PB*

MAP 2 Ref. 33

Nobrow
62 Great Eastern Street
Shoreditch EC2a 3QR
+44 (0)20 7033 4430
www.nobrow.net
Mon–Sat 11–6pm

Objects for use is about exactly that, beautifully made objects useful for many things by different cultures other than what they were originally intended for, such as a German Sauerkraut pot proving perfect for making Korean Kimchi. This tiny and uncluttered shop with simple chipboard shelving and a strong Japanese influence displays items with the aesthetic of a design museum, each piece showing how things can have many different uses, like heat pouches made from cherry stones, a by-product of jam and liquor which when heated stay warm for hours, along with bamboo charcoal, used for purifying water which can conveniently be ground down and used as fertiliser when used up. In addition to stools made from cardboard and complex wooden puzzles it just shows how simple useful things can be. *PB*

MAP 3 Ref. 43
Objects for use
15A Kingsland Road
Shoreditch E2 8AA
www.objectsforuse.com
Thur–Fri 12pm–7pm
Sat–Sun 11am–6pm

Shoreditch . **Home**

27

Finding the best of the best seems to be the theme here. There may be a few menswear stores in Shoreditch these days but none draws you in like **Present**. Whether it's the smell of fresh coffee from London based company, Square Mile, brewed by the 2009 world barista champion, or the scent of candles from France's oldest candle maker, Cire Trudon, for one reason or another your senses will compel you to take a look. A cathedral-like space with tall ceilings, it has custom-made, concrete-like floors and counter tops with pristine white display cabinets and aluminium shelving, all styled to perfection. They don't buy what they think will sell, they just buy what they think is the best, they reckon to have all bases covered. With clothes and bags from Comme Des Garcons and Heritage Research, sunglasses by Rayban, shoes by Vans and products from Aesop, they know a thing or two about quality. *PB*

MAP 2 Ref. 34

Present
140 Shoreditch High Street
Shoreditch E1 6JE
+44 (0)20 7033 0500
www.present-london.com
Mon–Fri 10.30–7pm
Sat 11–6.30pm
Sun 11–5pm

Conceived as a labour of love, everything you find here is hand made and the quality is impeccable. Crossing the boundary between fashion and lifestyle, **Soboye** has an Afro-centric or perhaps Afro-futuristic theme where many of the creations look towards Africa for ancestral inspiration, such as African headdress and Springbok* covered cushions, they even have the most divine and realistic fake fur throws you can imagine. There are beautiful hand beaded silks scarves and astonishingly sculptural high heels, too impressive to put into words. A great selection of colourful Eel skin purses and jewellery inspired and made by designers from India and China incorporating Magnetic Hematite and Lava along with bright pink Jade and florescent Perspex creates a particularly unusual collection. *PB*

*It's okay it's considered a pest in South Africa.

MAP 2 Ref. 37
Soboye
13 Calvert Avenue
Shoreditch E2 7JP
+44 (0)20 7729 3521
www.soboye.tumblr.com
Tue–Sun 12–6pm

-10%
Discount*

Purveyors of some of the finest underwear and staple clothing, British company **Sunspel** have been providing the most dapper English gentleman with cotton vests and boxer shorts for 150 years. The store on fashionable Redchurch Street is the personification of understated elegance and sophistication, with solid wood floors, teal coloured walls and straw boaters hung artfully on the wall, a nod to a long established client base. Sunspel specialise in jersey and Long Staple Egyptian Cotton grown only on the banks of the Nile. The recent addition of luxurious two-fold cotton highly prized around the world cements Sunspel as suppliers of pure luxury. They collaborate with many well known designers including Paul Smith and Margaret Howell, have a cameo in the famous Levi's 'launderette' advert where the model removes his jeans to reveal Sunspel boxer shorts and have produced bespoke t-shirts for Christian Bale in 'Batman The Dark Knight'. PB

MAP 2 Ref. 28

Sunspel
7 Redchurch Street
Shoreditch E2 7DJ
+44 (0)20 7739 9729
www.sunspel.com
Mon–Sat 11–7pm
Sun 12–6pm

Located in the heart of Shoreditch, a group of friends decided to open a store combining their passion for clothing, art and beer, henceforth **The Three Threads** was born. The name comes from a London beer first served at the Bell Brew-house on Curtain Road in the early 1700s. The theme is carried on through the sophisticated bar-style fit of the shop with low lighting and an old juke box making a nice touch. What clothing store can claim to have their own brand of beer brewed specially by a local micro brewery, free to customers? There is a strong graphic element to the shop with their sweet selection of graphic tees and ever changing T-shirt wall at the back of the store. Stocking an extensive collection of street wear for men from Edwin to Carhartt and only the best for women including Paul and Joe Sister and Opening Ceremony – the girls will certainly be happy too. *PB*

MAP 2 Ref. 32

The Three Threads
47-49 Charlotte Road
Shoreditch EC2A 3QT
+44 (0)20 7749 0503
www.thethreethreads.com
Mon–Sat 11–7pm
Sun 12–5pm

Spitalfields . *Fashion*

London's centre is sliding evermore east and those in the know say Redchurch Street is the hottest retail address in town. But you'd need a particular kind of thermal imaging to sense the outlets that are really pushing the mercury. There's no brash signage or loud advertising. It's more likely a quiet confidence in knowing that when you've got it right, they'll come. Stand opposite **Tracey Neuls** and watch passers-by stop in their tracks. Here at number 73 the chequer plate and graffiti of an urban landscape segue into a tableau of elegance demarcated only by a frame of neon pigment. This same sleight of hand engenders shoes that cause a similar reaction. A near miss, hesitation for a second glance, then a lingering intensity when you realise that something very different is going on. If true art is to conceal art then it's epitomised here. *GT*

MAP 2 Ref. 26
Tracy Neuls
73 Redchurch Street
Shoreditch E2 7DG
+44 (0)20 7018 0872
www.tn29.com
Tue–Sun 12–6pm
First Thursdays 12–9pm

From their base in an old button factory, close to Hoxton Square, what was once a mere fashion wholesalers is now one of Shoreditch's most fashionable stores. Home to some classy brands such as Designer's Remix, Twisted Vintage and By Zoe, the owners of **A142** hand-selected the collection from designers around the world, tastefully combining a few vintage pieces along with a collection of original artwork. This bright and airy space has a gallery vibe and lends itself as a perfect space to showcase their selection. They make putting the store together on a whim sound so easy, "we were already an office and showroom so putting in a front door wasn't a big stretch". It doesn't look that simple though, with custom sprayed lime-green clothes rails, scrap metal trestles, old stainless steel school lockers and paper butterflies creatively decorating the wall, it's certainly a classy showroom. Now with further ease they have moved a step closer to the high street opening a store in Old Spitalfields Market. *PB*

MAP 1 Ref. 6

A142
17 Lamb Street
Spitalfields E1 6EA
+44 (0)20 7377 8926
www.a142store.com
Mon–Sat 11–7pm
Sun 11–6pm

Spitalfields *Fashion*

A cheese shop just wouldn't be a cheese shop without the ripe scent of Camembert now would it? Parisian born owner, Alexandre has a long love affair with cheese. Having travelled the world exploring food, he came to London, finally opening his own shop. **Androuet** source cheese from all over the world, with 40% coming from Britain alone and all of which is bought directly from the producer. Selling only seasonal cheese they are the only shop in London who don't sell goats cheese in December or January. The restaurant, which has a selective seasonal menu featuring 'cheese of the week' dishes, features, come the winter, the traditional French favourites, Fondue and Raclette – rare to find outside of the Alps. Although mainly specialists in cheese they have enlisted the help of assistant sommelier to Gordon Ramsey to help choose the perfect selection of wines to compliment the diverse range. *PB*

MAP I Ref. 4

Androuet
Old Spitalfields Market
107b Commercial Street
Spitalfields E1 6BG
+44 (0)20 7375 3168
www.androuet.co.uk
Tue–Fri 11–8pm
Sat–Sun 11–7pm

Mad is the word that springs to mind when you walk into **Dolly Dare**, it's as if the shop has been transported all the way from Harajuku in Tokyo. Super high platforms and multi coloured shoes, crazy colourful dresses paired with elaborate tutus and diamante jewellery, it's all a cross between candy striper, Bridget Bardot and Japanese Lolita. With two main styles of dress designed and made in London, they come in all different types of fabric from tartan to sequins, floral and lace (although it's top secret where the designer finds her fabrics). The shop itself is equally eccentric, with black shagpile carpet, pink chandeliers, pink and white painted walls and shelves of old fashioned bottles of sweets, it's all very kitsch in the best sense of the word. *PB*

MAP 1 Ref. 3
Dolly Dare
107a Commercial Street
Spitalfields E1 6BG
+44 (0)20 7247 0472
www.dollydare.com
Mon–Sun 11am–8pm

Discount*

Purveyors of heritage clothing, at **DS Dundee** you will find only the very best by way of menswear. Going back to basics, they specialise in clothes designed to last in these throwaway times. Beautiful three piece suits, tweed blazers, shooting jackets, flat caps, cashmere scarves, the softest plaid shirts, sturdy yet elegant leather boots and pure wool sweaters all made from natural and hard wearing fabrics such as wool from Ireland, tweed form Scotland and cashmere from Mongolia. The collection is designed with true conviction and style using old milling techniques complete with the finest finishing touches, such as leather buttons and elbow pads. Attention to detail along with the highest level of comfort is paramount. The neatly edited selection takes true British classics giving them a modern urban appeal. PB

MAP I Ref. 5
DS Dundee
18 Lamb Street
Spitalfields E1 6EA
+44 (0)20 7241 2448
www.dsdundee.com
Mon–Fri 11–7pm
Sat–Sun 11–6pm

One of the stalwarts, **InSpitalfields** has succeeded in Spitalfields for what seems like forever, or at least, longer than all its near neighbours. From a market stall, through numerous pitches, to its present corner site, it's mirrored all the recent changes at this historic site with its own reincarnation as gift shop supreme. A note of warning: if you're pressed for time, Do Not Enter This Shop. The humour that runs through here like a stick of London-flavoured rock will have you dawdling in delight for hours. Animated by a hands-on staff who are fully involved in selecting the stock, their sensibilities as artists and designers in their own right translate into a thoughtful and engaging array of cards and products, often by new local talent. When you need a high-functioning present and you're dry of ideas, let their imaginations do the work for you. *GT*

MAP 1 Ref. 7
InSpitalfields
13 Lamb Street
Spitalfields E1 6EA
+44 (0)20 7247 2477
www.inspitalfields.co.uk
Everyday 10–7pm

Spitalfields . *Home*

Are you a fan of iconic furniture design but an original Le Corbusier is slightly out of your reach? **Interior Addict** specialise in excellent reproductions of the biggest names, Eero Saarinen, Verner Panton, Charles Eames, it's like a museum of iconic furniture design, including 1960's classics such as the ball chair by Eero Aarnio and lamps by Poul Henningsen. Having been a successful online shop, the owners were aware that with the abundance of online shops it was hard to trust the quality so they thought it important for customers to see the pieces in the flesh, to be able to sit in them and feel the good quality Italian leather. The large well lit space gives lots of room to walk around and visualise what would look good where in your home. *PB*

MAP 1 Ref. 1

Interior Addict

50–52 Commercial Street

Spitalfields E1 6LT

+44 (0)20 7377 1855

www.interioraddict.com

Mon–Sat 10am–6pm

Sun 11am–5pm

*Discount**

Keep Zero Gravity is an independent boutique solely distributing the ethereal creations of Greek designer Ioanna Kourbella. After Ioanna's success in Greece, the owners wanted to introduce her to the British market place. Her delicate and refined garments use as few seams and stitches as possible thereby creating clothes that are designed to fit the body perfectly. Ioanna grew up in Athens observing one of a kind, hand-knitted pieces produced in her father's workshop.

Her interest in tailoring developed and she went on to study fashion, costume and theatre design and was an early pioneer of using state-of-the-art textiles, made of natural fibres. The chic, simple design of the shop by a Greek theatre designer, offers a relaxing antidote to the colourful madness of Brick Lane. Additionally each month they invite a local artist to create an installation in the window as well as monthly design competitions in collaboration with Ioanna's designs. *PB*

MAP 1 Ref. 10

Keep Zero Gravity
20 Hanbury Street
Spitalfields E1 6QR
+44 (0)20 7247 5553
www.keepzerogravity.co.uk
Mon–Sun 11–7pm

Spitalfields | **Fashion**

The Lollipop Shoppe has a sweet eye for design! You might think you are in a kind of design sweet shop, a sweet shop selling beautifully designed products for the home, and I'm talking Verner Panton and Arne Jacobsen, not to mention Le Corbusier thrown in for good measure. Their theme is beautiful things. Classic and contemporary Scandinavian design seems to take precedence with Eames coathangers and Paul Henningsen lighting included. Concept pieces such as Piet Hein's 'super-elliptical' table where all sitters have equal importance and furniture, which experiments with bent wood and lamination are a joy for those with an interest in product design. It's not all big investment stuff though as the top floor is an eclectic selection of candles by Keith Haring, tinned sweets by Andy Warhol and multi-coloured headphones and watches interspersed with original artwork by Anthony Burrill and plastic pieces by Vasa, described as the most sensational colourist working in plastic today. *PB*

MAP 1 Ref. 8

The Lollipop Shoppe
10 Lamb Street
Spitalfields E1 6EA
+44 (0)20 7655 4540
www.thelollipopshoppe.co.uk
Mon–Sat 10–6pm
Sun 11-5pm

TeaSmith

It used to be that a cuppa down the market meant only one thing: the dark stew so beloved of builders, served bag in and likely with an aftertaste of polystyrene which might be only slightly relieved by the sludge of white sugar at the bottom of your take-away tumbler. Then came a gentleman from Scotland via the Chinatown tea houses of San Francisco and the self-service brew is no more. At **TeaSmith** they prepare earthy, fragrant Puers, Greens and Oolongs, each in a pot suited to the characteristics of the individual tea in a style that is as much theatre as function. Weary shoppers, jaded consumers, frightened bankers, Sunday morning survivors, I implore: allow the teasmiths to take you on a journey. Through woody, floral, roasted, sweet; tangy, fermented, smoky and smooth. Whatever your taste, to meander through this selection of East Asian leaves is to find new meaning in life. *GT*

MAP 1 Ref. 9
TeaSmith
6 Lamb Street
Spitalfields E1 6EA
+44 (0)20 7247 1333
www.teasmith.co.uk
7 days 11–6pm

Set slightly off the main thoroughfare away from the heart of uber cool Shoreditch is **Therapy**, a menswear store that certainly can hold its own on the style stakes. Decorated with much aplomb, large mirrors surrounded with light bulbs, walls plastered with comic book strips, not to mention the huge black and white slogans stating the likes of "Pretentious rhymes with twat". A blatant love of 1950's Americana comes through in their choice of labels including a corner of 1970's American Vintage.

The general idea is that upstairs are their main labels, classics such as Adidas Originals and Franklin & Marshall Black Label where as downstairs they have revolving sample sales featuring top notch labels. Womenswear is on its way so that's worth looking out for. *PB*

MAP I Ref. 2
Therapy
58 Commercial Street
Spitalfields E1 6LT
+44 (0)20 7247 8242
www.designertherapy.com
Mon–Wed 11–7pm
Thur–Fri 10–7pm
Sat–Sun 11–5pm

Are you looking for a gift but wine seems boring and a candle is unoriginal? Well what if the candle had Margaret Thatcher printed on it? And instead of wine how about handmade jam or honey from right here in London? Originality! is the theme of **123 Bethnal Green Road**. Created as a 'concept store' working with local artists, designers and food producers they stock both quirky, heritage and couture British brands while supporting young, home-grown talent. It covers four floors including gifts, jewellery and homewares on the ground floor, two floors dedicated to menswear and womenswear and 'The Bunker Café', serving freshly made, wholesome food at the bottom. They have it all covered. Selling a great selection of unusual things, from elegant jewellery fittingly titled the "Unholy Freaks Collection" to well-tailored clothes, 123 Bethnal Green Road does a great job championing weird and wonderful ideas. PB

MAP 2 Ref. 24

123 Bethnal Green Road
123 Bethnal Green Road
London E2 7DG
+44 (0)20 7729 8050
www.123bethnalgreenroad.co.uk
Mon–Sat 12–7pm
Sun 12–6pm

-10%

*Discount on clothes & jewellery**

All the dudes hang out at the beach. Surf's up around 6pm on an exhibition launch night. The beer flows and friends are made. Fortunately, it's a double yellow rather than a shore line along this particular beach and so, rain or shine, the party just washes over the kerb. Such social gatherings might perhaps be due to the launch of a new book at their pavement level shop or maybe a new show in **Beach** London's basement gallery where you'll find art that is ace, rad or sweet. It's a venture brand new to the scene, grown in part out of a web-based curatorial project featuring artists whose work might take the form of phone art, html code or ringtones. A limited edition A4 risograph print should cost you no more than the price of a few six packs. Awesome dude. *GT*

MAP I Ref. 16
Beach
20 Cheshire Street
Brick Lane E2 6EH
+44 (0)07590 370358
www.beachlondon.co.uk
Mon–Sun 12–6pm

The name **Double Store** derives from the fact that there are two stores on opposite sides of the street. One houses their studio downstairs where they produce their own line, 'Twins Diverse' creating pretty, modern-retro pieces inspired, yet not replicated from past decades like the twenties and fifties. Their garments keep to the essential lines, yet they invent new and brave shapes or they keep to the classic with an unusual flair added like smart trousers complete with little pleats on the hips. They use good quality, comfortable fabrics at reasonable prices applying the same rules when selecting other designers for the shop. Additionally they have handmade jewellery and bags from upcoming designers. The shop has a warm warehouse feel to it with soft lighting, large mirrors and cosy sofas creating a nice atmosphere. *PB*

MAP 1 Ref. 20
Double Store
194 Brick Lane
Brick Lane E1 6SA
+44 (0)20 7033 6633
www.doublestore.co.uk
Everyday 12–7pm

Brick Lane . *Fashion*

45

Dragana Perisic

Hailing from Eastern Europe, **Dragana Perisic** creates versatile and ultra-feminine, fanciful clothes from dresses to evening coats designed to be worn in different ways. With detachable sleeves that make an item wearable regardless of season, or a jacket that can be reversed making it appropriate for either day or evening wear, it is obvious she has fun inventing each piece. Her collection incorporates beautiful silk cushions and craft inspired jewellery made from handstitched fabric and silver. Using materials of the highest quality including translucent jerseys, leather, opulent brocades, floaty silks and super soft cotton in delicious and subtle colours she creates one-off timeless pieces. Her attention to detail is reflected in the dark wood floors, vintage velveteen cinema chairs and 70's furniture with Suffolk puffs, little scraps of silk gathered into flower like pieces which adorn her clothes and jewellery artfully placed in jars on the floor. *PB*

MAP 1 Ref. 17
Dragana Perisic
30 Cheshire Street
Brick Lane E2 6EH
+44 (0)20 7739 4484
www.draganaperisic.com
Tue–Fri 11–6pm
Sat–Sun 11–5pm

Discount on innovative handbags only*

Duke of Uke is a shop dedicated to all things Ukulele and what a selection of Ukulele's they have. Beautiful designs using different types of wood inspire you to buy one for no better reason than as decoration for on the wall. The shop was started by a big Ukulele aficionado as a community hub, yet due to the instruments' relatively recent surge in popularity has been doing very well every since and now offers lessons. After decades of somewhat obscurity the Ukulele has been rediscovered prompting it to be accepted back into the standard arsenal of instruments. Very popular with children and a nice change from the recorder it has proved equally loved amongst adults providing a great first instrument for those wanting to learn something new. PB

MAP 1 Ref. 19
Duke of Uke
88 Cheshire Street
Brick Lane E2 6EH
+44 (0)203 583 9728
www.dukeofuke.co.uk
Tue–Fri 12–7pm
Sat–Sun 11–6pm

Free tote bag with any purchase over £25*

It has to be said that one of the main attractions to a sprawling cosmopolitan city is that the best of the best is brought to your doorstep. With **Handmade Interiors** you needn't go much further than Brick Lane to find some of the loveliest hand-block and screen-printed textiles from cushion covers to cooking aprons and silk Turkish Hamam towels all the way from Turkey. Their main focus is on ethnic hand-printed products, all of which are printed in owner, Piyush's, mother's workshop back in Delhi and designed by Piyush himself. Limited edition ceramic pieces are interspersed with fragrant organic olive oil soaps and hand embroidered antique Hamam textiles from the Ottoman Empire. The simple interior of the shop shows off the delicate and beautiful designs with unique ceramics from British designers and a handwoven Turkish kaftan adorning the walls. *PB*

MAP I Ref. I4
Handmade Interiors
10 Cheshire Street
Brick Lane E2 6EH
+44 (0)20 7729 5704
www.handmade-interiors.co.uk
Tue–Sun 11–6pm

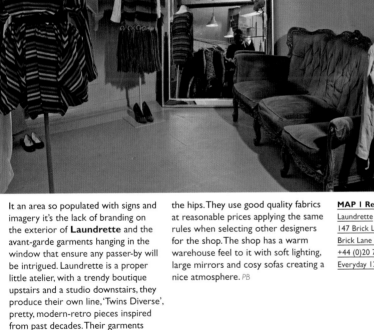

It an area so populated with signs and imagery it's the lack of branding on the exterior of **Laundrette** and the avant-garde garments hanging in the window that ensure any passer-by will be intrigued. Laundrette is a proper little atelier, with a trendy boutique upstairs and a studio downstairs, they produce their own line, 'Twins Diverse', pretty, modern-retro pieces inspired from past decades. Their garments introduce new and brave shapes with an unusual flair added like tailored trousers complete with little pleats on the hips. They use good quality fabrics at reasonable prices applying the same rules when selecting other designers for the shop. The shop has a warm warehouse feel to it with soft lighting, large mirrors and cosy sofas creating a nice atmosphere. *PB*

MAP 1 Ref. 21
Laundrette
147 Brick Lane
Brick Lane E1 6SA
+44 (0)20 7613 2553
Everyday 12–7pm

It started out as a hobby, a mere passion for all things old - but vintage clutter turned out to have quite a market for Jean-Luis, owner of chic and shambolic vintage shop **Le Grenier**. At first glance it may look like everything here is picked at random but many of the products here are collectibles and it is evident that he really knows his subject. He makes an effort to fill his shop with a mixture of what he likes but also what he knows people want. The collection is carefully sourced from flea markets all over England. Here you will find eclectic jewellery, exciting knick knacks and old record players interspersed with sixties ceramic sugar jars, full sets of tea cups piled onto classic English pieces, a Formica table or a G-plan dresser. Seventies lampshades mixed in with an old-fashioned type writer and an enamel bread bin complete the look. *PB*

MAP 2 Ref. 22

Le Grenier
146 Bethnal Green Road
Brick Lane E2 6DG
+44 (0)20 7790 7379
www.le-grenier.com
Mon–Fri 11–6pm
Wed Closed
Sat–Sun 10–6pm

If the glint of sunshine bouncing off the mirrored Perspex walls and three cats lounging on the counter don't instantly draw you in, then the stark white interior and ceiling installation of upturned milk bottles certainly will. With every space cleverly adorned with all kinds of seductive clutter from neon wallets and wristbands to framed illustrations and witty '5 second illustration' greetings cards, **Lik+Neon** places itself in a league of it's own. Fanzines by local artists and magazines celebrating people who look cool adorn one wall, with artist made jewellery, moustache cups, cassette tape wallets, surrealist socks and rare vintage sunglasses! and of course Mark Spitz's original design swimming trunks. No fashionable store in Shoreditch though would be complete without limited edition print and hand painted artist sweatshirts and over-sized t-shirts, hailing Lik Neon as the gift shop for the 'Museum of Cool'. *PB*

MAP I Ref. 13

Lik+Neon

106 Sclater Street

Brick Lane E1 6HR

+44 (0)20 7729 4650

www.likneon.com

Mon 12–7pm

Tue–Sat 11–7pm

Sun 11–6.30pm

Sixties inspired clothes shops come and go, usually because the novelty of dressing like an extra from Austin Powers wears off fairly quickly. **Mendoza** however is not about velvet and white knee high boots. Here you will find a serious menswear shop for those with a penchant for tailoring and classic Sixties Mod style. The Mod look was favoured by working class youths in the 1960's and encapsulated a very specific style of dress. Owner Leroy, a long established Mod himself realised a gap in the market for a look that despite the choice these days is hard to come by. Here you can walk in and walk out with an entirely new image. Mendoza will sort you out from head to toe, from Chelsea boots to tailored slacks in various pin stripes, tweed and chequered patterns not to mention the selection of short blouson style zipper jackets, turtle necks and ex-army parkas. *PB*

MAP 1 Ref. 12

Mendoza
158 Brick Lane
Brick Lane E1 6RU
+44 (0)20 7377 5263
www.mendozamenswear.com
Mon–Sun 12–6pm

Mar Mar Co are Mark and Marianne. They're designers. And when they're not designing for the likes of Tate Modern or the magical Museum of Childhood they turn their finely-tuned antennae to the work of other designers, whittling down to a finely edited collection of 'Everyware for Everyday'. So what makes the final cut for this outlet on Cheshire Street? Imagine a picnic in the garden. Well, you'd probably need a blanket, warm and woollen. A flask for your tea and a barbeque in a bucket. Perhaps an easy-to-assemble bird feeder so as not to waste the leftovers. A string bag to carry it all. And toys, pencils, even a small watering can to keep the restless amused. Then, like Woody Allen, you too can be at two with nature: enjoying the outdoors, while the great city roars comfortingly around. *GT*

MAP 1 Ref. 15

Mar Mar Co
16 Cheshire Street
Brick Lane E2 6EH
+44 (0)20 7729 1494
www.marmarco.com
Thur–Sat 12–5.30pm
Sun 11–5pm

"We want to sell clothes that people will be wearing in 10 years". In a time where everything is disposable this is a nice sentiment. Stockists of some exceptionally well crafted men's apparel including Barbour, Libertine Libertine and Sebago, **Number Six** is at the forefront of menswear stores. Here you can buy everything from the toes up - shoes, socks, coats, hats, bags and sunglasses and all in the best brands. The store itself is a stylish fit with industrial pipes, 70's furniture, antique cabinets, stag's antlers and framed butterflies – a nod to the ever fashionable Victoriana of East London. It's the bright green astro-turf effect floor, which sets this menswear store apart from the rest though. A slight afterthought, as the floor was apparently in a bit of state, it's nothing short of genius creating the perfect environment for men where it might almost be like shopping on a football pitch. *PB*

MAP 1 Ref. 11
Number Six
6 Dray Walk
91–95 Brick Lane
Brick Lane E1 6QL
+44 (0)20 7392 9686
www.numbersixlondon.com
Tue–Fri 10.30–6.30pm
Sat–Sun 11–6.30pm

It all started when the owner Melody bought an old map for a friend salvaged from a French schoolroom that she realised the mass appeal of such special items. **Tools** is a treasure box of beautiful things, it's like the studio of an eccentric collector and if it wasn't for Melody, many of these things would not have managed to survive. A collection of colourful and unusual maps with quirky graphics along with educational wall charts of lizards, some of which date back to before the second world war adorn the walls. Old cabinets with shelves and drawers full of precious things such as old and elaborate buttons, antique negatives, little diaries from the 1930's and gorgeous vintage fabrics are bound to inspire all those with a curiosity for the past. *PB*

MAP I Ref. 18

Tools
32 Cheshire Street
Brick Lane E2 6EH
+44 (0)7952 184 711
www.toolslondon.wordpress.com
Mon–Sat 11am–6pm
Sun 10–6pm
Tue Closed

"I think of a letter and then mark around the thought…It may be easy to think of one letter, but to think also of its twenty-five relations which with it form the alphabet and so to mark around them that they will combine in complete harmony and rhythm with each other and with all – that is the difficult thing, the successful doing of which constitutes design." So said Frederic Goudy, whose designs have survived the transition from galleys through typewriters to the ubiquitous computer. But **Type** on Bethnal Green Road isn't a museum to print. Rather it draws on the culture and history of print technologies and incorporates physical elements from these and other redundant industries into a new aesthetic which finds its form in hand-crafted furniture and lighting. Low tech processes and custom-built objects are fetishised as an antidote to an increasingly digital and homogenised world. Amen to that! Carriage return. *GT*

MAP 2 Ref. 23
Type
138 Bethnal Green Road
Brick Lane E2 6DG
+44 (0)20 3489 7644
www.typeeast.com
Mon (By appointment)
Tue–Sun 9–6pm

Push pass the woollen slip of large stitches that masquerades as a door sign and enter a rose-scented fairytale of textile and text, matter and madness. Walls are papered with fading stories, china teacup candles waft sweet warmth and handmade cards and corsages clutter every surface. **Jessie & Buddug** are art school friends who employ their Welsh language and heritage of romantic tradition to seductive effect in work that embraces theatrical installations such as Selfridges' Alice in Wonder Room, their individual fine art practices and all the offerings in this eponymous shop: handmade albums for your photos and ephemera, customised vintage linen, lace and wool garments, enamelled jewellery engraved with favourite phrases and the loveliest Lovespoons, crafted from combinations of wood, metal and fabric. Choose their gift tokens or commission a piece from the bespoke wedding range to make someone feel very special. *GT*

MAP 4 Ref. 56

Jessie Chorley & Buddug
158a Columbia Road
E2 7RG
+44 (0)7704708577
+44 (0)7708921550
www.jessiechorley.com
www.buddug.com
Tue–Fri (By appointment)
Sat 12–5pm Sun 9–4pm

As with a walk through botanical gardens, navigating a path round **L'Orangerie** requires some limber moves. Arranged along tall tables interposed with bay trees is a heady, clinking menagerie of colour, form and overhanging jewellery. Brush past fellow pickers in the slinky aisles and try not to catch your hair on a butterfly brooch or leafy earrings. It's an approach to selling that will infuriate or intoxicate. Those who surrender easily to the resinous slick of a bauble, clip or ring will appreciate the affordable prices and eccentric aesthetic. The overwhelmed should escape to the spacious calm of the lower level. Here the reward is a choice of kilim textiles, Panamas and floppy-brimmed sun hats à la Francoise Gilot, whose look encapsulates the style of L'Orangerie. *GT*

MAP 4 Ref. 58

L'Orangerie
162 Columbia Road
E2 7RG
+44 (0)7525 004300
Sat 10–5pm
Sun 8.30–5.30pm

West End girls with East End lives could do worse than refresh their wardrobe at **Marcos and Trump**, the boutique with an eye on both worlds. The mission statement is to provide a style that will endure both seasonal change and financial fluctuation as well as the crosstown flow of a London life. How to achieve this? With a mainstay of labels such as Peopletree, Full Circle and Darling, alongside Melissa for shoes and occasional others who provide a nod to the more fleeting phases of fashion. There's a strong evening and partywear bias which allows for the very ingenious range of Fashion First Aid accessories, designed to deal with boobs that just won't sit up, lie flat, or do whatever it is exactly THAT dress requires of them. Ultimately, it's a girls world. *GT*

MAP 4 Ref. 55

Marcos and Trump
146 Columbia Road
E2 7RG
+44 (0)20 7739 9008
www.marcosandtrump.com
Thu–Fri 12–6pm
Sat 11–6pm Sun 9–4pm

Discount*

Milagros

This is the shop that vies with the market for colour, and comes out on top. As sure as the bees fly to the flowers outside many will find themselves drawn to the florid interior of this Mexican microcosm. Stunningly incongruous, **Milagros** has everything you wanted to buy on holiday but weren't sure would survive the plane journey home. Jet-lagged customers aren't unknown. Saints, skeletons, virgins and wrestlers all make an appearance alongside the votive paintings, handcrafted paper cuts and bubbly recycled glassware. The latest addition is a range of baskets, immaculately hand-woven from galvanised wire and polythene. They come in a variety of colours and four standard forms but, as with the ceramic tiles, can be commissioned in any other size or colour, such is the value of an independent outlet that has a personal relationship with all its suppliers. *GT*

MAP 4 Ref. 53
Milagros
61 Columbia Road
E2 7RG
+44 (0)20 7613 0876
www.milagros.co.uk
Mon–Sat (By appointment)
Sun 9–4pm

Is it a gallery or a café? No, it's a café and a coffee bar. A gallery sandwich? Oh, I don't know. Whatever. **StartSpace** has not one, but two coffee outlets with a gallery space in between, and it's all extremely pleasant. Pick up a latte from the skinniest slip of a stand, a mere doorway wide, then take a wander through the grey-washed interior to reflect on the paintings. Figurative and abstract work, from contemporary mid-career artists, is the staple. There's usually a group show, occasionally some sculpture and always a few select pieces of applied art. The contrast with the frenzy of the market couldn't be more marked and it's a truly refreshing and relaxed environment in which to appreciate artwork. By the time you reach the veranda with its kitchen café your heart rate should have dropped a few beats and it'll be time for another coffee. *GT*

MAP 4 Ref. 54

StartSpace
150 Columbia Road
E2 7RG
+44 (0)20 7729 0522
www.startspace.co.uk
Sat 12–6pm
Sun 8–3pm

Not a place for the diabetically inclined, **Suck & Chew** even smells dangerous. The sugared air taunts with essences of banana, kola, aniseed and custard. If you can't remember the last time you had a pink flying saucer stuck to the roof of your mouth, your tongue turned evil with a Black Jack or your jaw locked down with a Fruit Salad then make haste to Suck and Chew, the shop that time forgot. All the old favourites are here and the jars are just as big as ever. An irreverent humour flavours the décor and the imaginative employment of original coronation mugs and technicolor vintage tins for packaging guarantees some rare and very good value gifts. Can't make it to the shop? Buy online. Can't bear to leave? Invite them to pop-up at your office party, birthday or wedding. Willy Wonka, eat your heart out! *GT*

MAP 4 Ref. 51
Suck & Chew
130 Columbia Road
E2 7RG
+44 (0)20 8983 3504
www.suckandchew.co.uk
Thu–Fri 12–6pm
Sat 12–5pm
Sun 9–4.30pm

Turn your green fingers pink with pleasure. By popular demand **The Powder Room**, in all its candy-striped glory, has landed safely in the East End. These former flying doctors of the beauty world are now firmly established as a fixed entity on Columbia Road, albeit at weekends only for the time being. All you have to decide is how much time-out you can take in this palace of pampering. Nail treatments are 15, 30 or 40 minutes in duration and with prices starting at £20 you'll still have change

for flowers. Make-up, new lashes or the latest 'Up Do' can be administered pretty swiftly too. Prices include tea and biscuits which make it a very affordable break from a breathless weekend. But if glamour is your weekday vice, don't forget the Soho branch in Marshall street – open Monday to Saturday. GT

MAP 4 Ref. 52
The Powder Room
136 Columbia Road
E2 7RG
+44 (0)844 879 4928
www.thepowderpuffgirls.com
Sat 12–6pm
Sun 10–4pm

Columbia Road . **Beauty**

"I say, what's this?" Here among the 1953 Schoolfriend Annual, the wooden badminton racquet that weighs like concrete and the battered tartan Thermos is, well, everything but Grandma's kitchen sink. This one-woman collection, gathered over a lifetime's obsession with house sales, fêtes and car boots really is vintage heaven. She did it so you don't have to. Just make sure you get here before it sells out – the Americans have been bulk-buying. Cross-stitch scenes of The Last Supper and kitsch landscapes with pink skies are winners, as are the acres of textiles, tea sets and bone-handled cutlery. The piles of publications feature worthy wartime recipes, splendid knitting patterns plus a whole lot of horticulture. And the last word in teatime must be **Vintage Heaven**'s Cakehole café, a wholly retro delight. *GT*

MAP 4 Ref. 50

Vintage Heaven

82 Columbia Road

E2 7QB

+44 (0)1277 215968

www.vintageheaven.co.uk

Mon–Thu (By appointment)

Fri 12–5pm

Sat 12–6pm

Sun 8.30–5.30pm

Determined not to work in a shop but wanting to have a shop anyway, two girls with a similar philosophy and a love of antiques decided to create a studio doubling as a showroom displaying their creations. Resembling a room from a stately home, decorated with beautiful and eclectic pieces of furniture salvaged from a friends eccentric relative, **Wall & Jones** is the creation of Sara-Jane Chase and Ali Wall, both independent designers. Gorgeous jewellery made from quirky antique pieces reassembled into whimsical creations each complete with a tag outlining the item's history are displayed alongside theatrical designs by Ali Wall who uses sumptuous vintage fabrics and tapestries to create one off garments. Downstairs is a decadent atelier complete with baroque and imaginative fittings, providing a rare treat where customers can see the designers at work. *PB*

MAP 4 Ref. 59

Wall and Jones
340 Hackney Road
E2 7RH
+44 (0)20 7729 6768
www.wallandjones.com
www.ali-wall.com
www.halo-jones.com
Wed–Sun 11–7pm

Columbia Road . *Fashion*

Wawa's bright and tactile showroom, full of colour, is the workspace of bespoke furniture maker Richard Ward. Specialising in seating, his signature Soho Two sofa is a diminutive and elegant two-seater and the most recent design, Bay, was devised to fit the bay windows so typical of London homes. As with all his pieces, proportions can be modified to fit any space: depth, height and length are all variables, even the profile of the cushions attracts his meticulous attention to detail. In a charming acknowledgment, new commissions are often named for the client – thus Yasmin, Oscar and Dorothee, each with its own distinctive character. The shop sells other homewares, mostly by UK designers but it's worth visiting for the extensive fabric department alone, with its strong emphasis on texture and featuring the likes of Kenzo, Lelievre and Sahco among other classic names. *GT*

MAP 4 Ref. 57

Wawa

1 Ezra Street

E2 7RH

+44 (0)20 7729 6768

www.wawa.co.uk

Weekdays (By appointment)

Sun 10–2.30pm

Rueing the demise of Borders and suffering cold turkey for your fashion magazine fix? **Artwords Bookshop** can ease your pain. Seven days a week, Artwords offers the full extended qwerty of contemporaryvisualculture with thwacking great style mags making up a serious chunk of their selection. True there's no coffee-shop but with so many lining the street outside only the meanest would moan. Hackney is said to have the greatest concentration of artists in Europe and Broadway Market is surely an artery from the heart of this artistic community. Galleries, studios and workshops abound. To eavesdrop the in-shop conversations is to understand how the publications here reflect the knowledge base of the area. There's much to be found in this collection that isn't at Amazon but if your desire is arcane beyond their considerable ken, any omission can be ordered for you. You need never leave Hackney again. *GT*

MAP 6 Ref. 62

Artwords Bookshop
20–22 Broadway Market
E8 4QJ
+44 (0)20 7923 7507
www.artwords.co.uk
Mon–Fri 10.30–6.30pm
Sat 10–6pm
Sun 10.30–7pm

Mary Poppins would find much to approve of in **Black Truffle**. And if you weren't practically perfectly shod before, you too will have no excuse once you've found this place. Run by a shoemaker, in tandem with an international school of shoemaking, there's no question of anything being less than top quality. From lace-up boots through Oxfords and brogues to Mary-Janes, peep-toes, espadrilles and pumps; for the discerning customer they've got it covered. Neither run-of-the-mill nor faddish there's a distinct brand aesthetic that's gently quirky, played out in the finest leather and cloth, fancy uppers stitched down firmly to quality soles. With so much attention to detail on the main event you could forgive a slacking in the sidelines, but no, here you'll find smocks and shirts, accessories and jewellery, all meeting the same criteria. The final flourish is the oddest gift shelf. I'll let you discover. *GT*

MAP 6 Ref. 61
Black Truffle
4 Broadway Market
E8 4PH
+44 (0)20 7923 9450
www.blacktruffle.com
Tue-Fri 11–6pm
Sat 10–6pm
Sun 12–6pm

The **Climpson & Sons** east London coffee revolution is brewing away just a stone's throw from their cafe in Broadway Market. Each new roast giving away their location with heady aromas. A daily scene sees Danny Davies (Director) tasting while Matthew Ho (barista trainer) gets excited while 'cupping' (must be the caffeine), the way each roast is individually tasted for consistency and flavour anomalies. While Ryan (head roaster) assisted by trainee Regan, oversees the latest beans out of the roaster. A typically busy scene at Climpson who pride themselves in their scientific and precise hands-on approach to specialty coffee. They don't use commodity coffees but prefer to source beans from single estates where the nuances in the bean reflect the territory they come from. Roasting small quantities of all flavours and bespoke blends. The word coffee doesn't cover it but hey don't take our word for it, discover your favourite blend with a bun at the cafe. *MS*

MAP 6 Ref. 68

Climpson & Sons
67 Broadway Market
E8 4PH
+44 (0)20 7254 7199
www.climpsonandsons.com
Mon–Fri 8–5pm
Sat 8.30–5pm
Sun 8.30–4pm

According to my dictionary a 'fabrication' is constructed or manufactured from prepared components. **Fabrications** on Broadway Market is woven of the strands, shop, studio and workshop classroom. It's good to know this before you arrive. You might otherwise wonder what exactly it is that you've encountered – this colourful cube being little more than a shop-front for a multitude of activities focused on sustainability. Cocooned in haberdashery, British wools, publications on knitting and sewing, eco home-wares, gifts and some well-worth-a-rummage off-cuts bins, regular craft classes in all manner of textile techniques take place in the main space. Downstairs is the studio. Here 'Up-cycling' dominates all practice, from proprietor Barley Massey's textile design business, to the Remember Me service whereby your long-loved but aged garment, saggy and loose at the seams, can be commissioned for revival as a quilt, artwork or other textile worth treasuring for yet another lifetime. *GT*

MAP 6 Ref. 65

Fabrications

7 Broadway Market

E8 4PH

+44 (0)20 7275 8043

www.fabrications1.co.uk

Tue–Fri 12–5pm

Sat 10–5.30pm

Sun: workshops

Free loyalty card stamp*

Narrow as a ship's galley, **Fin & Flounder** is replete with the essentials for your fish dinner, the back wall lined with condiments and herbs, the counter bearing baskets of lemons. Newly licenced, they now feature a sensibly slim selection of predominantly Italian wines. Anxieties can be left at the door as the management supply fish only from Marine Stewardship Council preferred sources. Where the criteria can't be met they simply won't stock an item, preferring instead to market 'bycatch', the often disregarded by-product of a fishing excursion. This makes for a far more interesting shopping experience than at the supermarket where the packets are the same shape every day. Under its blue awning, the sluiced and tiled interior sings of the sea and fishmongers of a bygone age. These nostalgic notes are no accident as the team delivers a proper service and can advise on preparation and recipes. *GT*

MAP 6 Ref. 69

Fin & Flounder
71 Broadway Market
E8 4PH
+44 (0)7838 018 395
www.finandflounder.com
Tue–Fri 10–6.30
Sat 9–5pm
Sun 11–4pm

Broadway Market. **Food**

71

A bit of fluffy taxidermy, in the cheery light of day, can sure pull on the purse strings. Throw in a birthday poo card, a few meteorite shards and Susanna's front-bottom, forever foxy in formaldehyde (yours for £125) and you'll definitely win the prize for best present. However, one might want to think twice before releasing anything from the Pandora's box that is the creepy canal-side cellar of **The Last Tuesday Society**. Here below the shop and art gallery lie the motley and the monstrous, things of fact and fiction and the "doctored back end of a deer". Hours may be lost in this underworld of provocation where Gary Glitter, Enid Blyton and Mr. Robertson's golliwogs seem entirely at home amongst the relics in this, the only place ever known to promote the purchase of a fur jacket with the assurance that it's the skin of a 'long-dead' animal. *GT*

MAP 6 Ref. 63

The Last Tuesday Society
11 Mare Street
Hackney E8 8RP
+44 (0)20 7998 3617
www.thelasttuesdaysociety.org
Wed–Sun 12–7pm

Named for the Gainsbourg song, welcome to 'mouth-watering' the café. The food and the tunes here are global in their reach, although, like the sausages in the deli, with a distinct North African flavour. This is the joint that feeds the food stars, catering recently for Nigel Slater and his Simple Suppers team, so it's worth staying for more than just a coffee. Fresh produce is mostly sourced locally or at least from within Europe, never air-freighted and served seasonally. The deli and grocery shelves proffer British basics alongside continental goodies and the wine racks are the pride of the proprietor. Established in 2004 and since moving from smaller premises along the way **l'eau à La Bouche** has grown its clientele to fill the bigger space, and then some. Even on a grey day there's enough of a cosmopolitan gaggle at the tables outside to shame any Parisian equivalent. *GT*

MAP 6 Ref. 66

l'eau à La Bouche
35-37 Broadway Market
E8 4PH
+44 (0)20 7923 0600
www.labouche.co.uk
Mon–Fri 8.30–7pm
Sat 8.30–5pm
Sun 9–5pm

Nr. Broadway Market . **Food**

Pragmatically positioned on what must be London's most biked thoroughfare, is the lovely, so lofty **Lock 7**. With its high ceilings, raw concrete floor and Scandi style you might just want to move in. This pit stop of repair and sustenance is like no other and the dominant feature, it has to be said, is girls. Run by girls and mostly staffed by girls, its great popularity can be attributed to the good nature, sound advice and genuine commitment to bike health of the team. These local business ingénues who started up with nothing more than a desire to keep good bicycles off the scrap pile are now at the helm of a thriving enterprise that sells great coffee, food to beat any dedicated outlet, every part and accessory you could possibly need - and the multi-coloured versions you probably don't — with quick turnaround services at entirely reasonable prices. *GT*

MAP 6 Ref. 60

Lock 7

129 Pritchards Road

Broadway Market E2 9AP

+44 (0)20 7739 3042

www.lock-7.com

Tue–Sat 8–6pm

Sun 10–6pm

"A Micro brewery that rolls up the door for some great beer, food and events." Ian Burgess (right) and brewer's mate David Dodkin measure the temperature in the mash tun the stage of the beer brewing process where the sugars are extracted from the malt. **London Field's Brewery** believe in sourcing and making the most of ingredients available today, using British and new world hops while sticking to tried and tested slow brewing techniques. Beers range from traditional style English ales,

lager filtered and unfiltered packed with flavour based on what the best European brewers have mastered over the years, as well as crafted ales taking influences from American and antipodean styles. Try them all at one of their weekend events. *MS*

MAP 6 Ref. 70

London Fields brewery
374 Helmsley place
Hackney E8 3SB
+44 (0)20 7254 0008
www.londonfieldsbrewery.co.uk
(By Appointment only unless
attending one of the events)

Our Patterned Hand might better be called unpatterned so little is repeated at this hip haberdasher. Established by a deserter from the fashion industry, jaded with the increasing standardisation so prevalent in popular fashion, most items are the antithesis of the mass-produced. Aside from the full extent of sewing supplies there's a rainbow of dyes and fabric paints and a selection of fabrics to rival any West End specialist.
The stock comprises limited edition digital prints from Italy, one-off lengths of kimono fabric exquisitely hand-worked and prints from local designers, all in natural fibres. Buttons are made of bone, paper and plant fibres – no plastic – and if you don't quite know what to do with all this wonderful stuff then you'll be welcome in the workshop downstairs where someone is on hand to help with your tailoring or customising project. *GT*

MAP 6 Ref. 67
Our Patterned Hand
49 Broadway Market
E8 4RE
+44 (0)20 7812 9912
www.ourpatternedhand.co.uk
Tue–Fri 10–6pm
Sat 10–5pm
Sun 12–5pm

-10%
Discount*

Halfway between the grasses of London Fields and the wildflowers of the Regent's canal flourishes a variety of colour and foliage that isn't so dissimilar. Culled from across the British isles — gardens commercial and private — it's to be found at **Rebel Rebel**, the standalone flower shop that has said a firm 'no' to the standardised arrangements required by the international delivery folk and created a style that regularly attracts commissions from TV companies, fashion houses and arts institutions. Fortunately this high profile activity hasn't stopped them continuing to offer the simplest pleasures to the casual passer-by. Bestsellers are humble cornflowers, at three quid a bunch. Other favourites being dahlias, sweetpeas, delphiniums and jasmine. Anything can be bought as a single stem and frequent visits will reward the enthusiast as the seasons are marked by an ever-changing stock that is subject to the wanderings of the British climate. *GT*

MAP 6 Ref. 64
Rebel Rebel
5 Broadway Market
E8 4PH
+44 (0)20 7254 4487
www.rebelrebel.co.uk
Tue—Fri 10–6pm
Sat 9–5pm

BOROUGH WIN

Wilton Way Café 63 Wilton Way E8 1BG
(Home to London Fields Radio)
www.londonfieldsradio.com | **Map 6 Ref. 72**

LFR

London Fields Radio

Borough Wines 67 Wilton Way E8 1BG
www.boroughwines.com | **Map 6 Ref. 74**

ON A

Toppers of Hackney 65 Wilton Way E8 1BG
www.toppersofhackney.com | **Map 6 Ref. 73**

-10%

Toppers discount

e **Other Side of the Pillow** 6 Wilton Way E8 1BG
w.theotherothersideofthepillow.blogspot.com | **Map 6 Ref. 71**

Those who hail from Wilton Way...

Tired of travelling the world for the Norwegian tourist board, Egil decided it was time to settle down. All set for Camden (the only place in London he'd heard of) when he was told by a man from Bethnal Green the only place to live in London was Hackney. He's a real lover of English pub culture "in England everyone socialises every day of the week, the pub is like their living room". This is exactly how it feels in **The Kenton Pub**, home at once. Every night is different. Monday is film night, Tuesday a quiz night, Wednesday live music or comedy, Thursday is 'Ladies night' with a jumble sale, nail decoration, cakes & cocktails and of course Fri/Sat has DJs. On Sunday it's back for a lazy all day Sunday roast. On Fridays between 6 and 7pm try your luck against Egil in a game of 'sissors, paper, stone', if you win you get the round for half price. Look out for the moose his grandad shot in 1971. Deserved winner of the 2010 "newcomer in London award" We're glad he chose Hackney. MS

MAP 6 Ref. 84

The Kenton Pub
38 Kenton Road
Hackney E9 7AB
+44 (0)20 8533 5041
www.kentonpub.co.uk
Mon–Thur 4–11pm
Fri–Sat 4–12am
Sun 12–11pm

Dutch artist Karin Janssen is Well Street's newest arrival. Seeking an energetic vibrant neighbourhood that could inspire her she chose Hackney. "I lived in Brazil for a while and in many ways it's actually a lot like there! Lots of contrasts and different cultures. I like to immerse myself in a completely different environment to my own upbringing in Holland. Hackney feels real, not polished." **Karin Janssen Project Space** is not just a gallery, but also a networking space for artists. "Artists can find their 'artist's life' quite a lonely, isolating experience, often only meeting new people at gallery openings – the networking events help them discover other artists and share their experiences". *MS*

MAP 6 Ref. 81

Karin Janssen Project Space
213 Well Street
Hackney E9 6QU
+44 (0)20 85 250 294
www.karinjanssen.com
During Exhibitions
Wed–Sat 12–6pm
and by appointment

Hackney . **Art**

Wells butchers

Wells butchers, now in it's third generation, is a firm favourite of Well Street in Hackney. First opening in January 1931 and hardly closing since, it predates anything else on the street. It's longevity a testament to their success even surviving the establishment of one of the earliest Tesco's on the corner opposite in 1970 – we can't help thinking this must have been a nice junction before the arrival of Tesco. Father and son, Alan(right) and Paul(middle), now run the shop serving 'made to order' cuts to happy locals, pubs and restaurants. Long may they continue. *MS*

MAP 6 Ref. 82

Wells butchers
211 Well Street
Hackney E9 6QU
+44 (0)20 8985 4602
www.wellsbutchers.co.uk
Mon–Sat 7.30–6.30pm

Gourmet! That's one word I can't say enough when speaking of this exquisite little deli. **L'epicerie @56** is like a little slice of France with a delectable selection of pastries from Amandines, Clafoutis, Florentines and Macaroons to good old chocolate brownies. And the bread! Tangy sour dough and fluffy baguettes, delicious! They stock all the best ingredients, olive oil, organic grains and flour piled up in rustic baskets on the floor, alongside sardines in brightly coloured tins, multicoloured lollipops and sweets in old-fashioned jars. They serve coffee, hot chocolate and a few freshly made sandwiches using warm Ciabatta, Focaccia and scrumptious hams and cheeses. There are a few spots to sit although it's mainly takeaway for those in need of their daily steaming latte and divine viennoiserie. *PB*

Map 6 (Off the page)
L'épicerie @56
56 Chatsworth Road
Hackney E5 0LS
+44 (0)20 7503 8172
www.lepicerie56.com
Mon–Fri 8.30–7pm
Sat–Sun 8.30–5.30pm

Free coffee on purchase over £10* (Weekdays only)

Let's just say that this little bar (for want of a better word) and named after the owner, is something everyone with any penchant for weirdness needs to experience. As **Lumiere** points out, it looks like a juice bar set up by the Madam of a brothel. That helps explain the flocked wallpaper, flickering fake candles and disco ball then. Although they don't want to put a label on what kind of a place it is, they do serve incredible smoothies, milkshakes and cocktails generally made, "as we go along" and named after local streets such as Columbia Cucumber and Glenarm Slipper. Downstairs is warren of little rooms with a charming bathroom, complete with sea noises, because as Lumiere points out "you always remember a place by the bathroom!". *PB*

Map 6 (Off the page)
Lumiere
88 Chatsworth Road
Hackney E5 0LS
+44 (0)7914 670 285 (Text only)
www.lumierelondon.blogspot.com
7 Days – times vary

Nixie designs clothes so adorable it will make you want to have kids just so you can dress them! Everything is designed onsite, the cupboards bursting with vintage fabrics and dress patterns give the shop a lovely haphazard appeal. All the garments from miniature pantaloons to silk skirts and little wool coats are made from re-cycled fabric and re-conditioned wool, nothing goes to waste, if there is leftover ribbon it will be made into hairclips and jewellery. The current collection is made up solely from vintage silk scarves, a process that causes quite a headache, yet so lovely it merely prompts customers to whine "why can't you make this in my size?", thus a one off capsule collection was created, alongside a neatly edited collection of vintage clothes for adults just to keep everyone happy. *PB*

Map 6 (Off the page)
Nixie
92a Chatsworth Road
Hackney E5 0LS
+44 (0)7970 073584
www.nixieclothing.com
Mon–Sat 11–6pm

Since 2008 **Hackney WickED** continued its mission to fuel London's thriving East End art scene showcasing work from local and international artists through galleries, open studios, temporary exhibitions, pop up spaces, site-specific installations, a music stage and events throughout Hackney Wick and Fish Island. The festival attracts visitors from all over Europe. The Hackney WickED collective exhibits throughout the year through pop-up exhibitions. "It was a way of demonstrating the existing artist culture in Hackney Wick" before the area becomes gentrified as a result of Olympic development. We wanted to express the vibrancy of the area under our own control" says Laura May Lewis, one of the directors of the festival. "Hackney Wick is a DIY culture" "We want to keep the festival's non-commercial integrity - which wouldn't be possible without the many volunteers who give up their time to make the festival work". Laura May Lewis, who came for the natural light, quiet and low rents. Can it last with all the olympic development?, we'll see. *MS*

MAP 5 Ref. 87

Hackney WickED festival (last weekend in July)
Hackney Wick E9
www.hackneywickedfestival.co.uk

Directors of Hackney WickED:
Jess Hudsley, Joanna Hughes, Anna Maloney
Laura May Lewis, Simon Rueben-White

(From left) Maree Featherstonhaugh (Production Assistant), Fabio Scarpa (Music Director), Laura May Lewis (Director), Ed Metcalf (Production Manager), photographed in front of Hackney Wick's very own 'HollyWick Sign' made by Laura May Lewis above **Hackney Pearl Map 5**

Originally a shell of a building housing a squat, when Rebecca and Neil first visited, they had a police escort due to a recent stabbing right in front of the door. Starting out as an affordable space for their own work the Stour Space has grown to become an art hub on the 'Fish Island' side of Hackney Wick with monthly exhibitions promoting art, markets supporting local trade, and educational and outreach projects dealing with developments in the local area.
The Counter café moved into Stour Space in April this year. Café by day and tapas restaurant (Counter Soir) by night. With great food and space to feed the surrounding creatopolis; the two enterprises have found a perfect match. Rebecca is mindful of the fact that with the olympic torch now illuminating the area of Wick, all underground activity has been forced out of the shadows and with the accompanying rise in investment and rising popularity of the area there's the risk of a Shoreditch style mutation. MS

MAP 5 Ref. 86

The Counter
7 Roach Road
Hackney Wick E3 2PA
+44 (0)7834 275 920
www.thecountercafe.co.uk
Café
Mon–Fri 7.45–5pm
Sat/Sun 9–5pm
Counter Soire (tapas)
Thu–Sun 6.30pm–late

Despite no official support they have established a quite fantastic space serving the local area. **Stour Space** like to work with the local community, who are feeling under represented with the amount of new money being spent in the area – new nightclubs, bars and modern art studios that threaten to undercut the studios already here. One of the great attractions of Wick was always it's affordability which allowed the freedom to work and live with fewer of the pressures of the commercial world. Unusual space, innovative business, theaters, music nights and parties in an ultimately previously remote location cultivated a dynamic cultural scene in the area – all of which may not survive large new development, town planners and general meddling and bureaucracy associated with it. Evidenced by the sight of traffic wardens in Wick. *MS*

MAP 5 Ref. 85

Stour Space
7 Roach Rd
Hackney Wick E3 2PA
+44 (0)20 8985 7827
www.stourspace.co.uk
Mon–Wed 8–5pm
Thu–Sun 8–1am

Hackney Wick . **Art**

It's all here, plus beer. Owner Andrew spotted a yawning chasm in the market and filled it with wines from around the world. Smaller boutique producers are strongly featured and on any visit you can taste up to 32 wines from the Enomatic machine. **Bottle Apostle** will track your purchases for you, enabling you to repeat your favourites and allowing them to propose new ones, of which they have roughly 15 per week. Within a year of opening they have acquired a loyal clientele perhaps seduced by the sociability of their weekly events: nights of German wines served with Vietnamese flavours from neighbouring Namo or suggestions for fish with a lesson in prep from the local fishmonger. It's hard in this most gentle patch of London to escape the village shop vibe and these blow-ins are no exception. The team are welcoming, unpretentious and friendly, their enthusiasm engaging. *GT*

MAP 6 Ref. 76

Bottle Apostle

95 Lauriston Road

Victoria Village E9 7MJ

+44 (0)20 8985 1549

www.bottleapostle.com

Tue–Fri 12–9pm

Sat 10–8pm

Sun 10–6pm

The traditional hierarchies of value are laid to waste in the jewellery of Julia Cook. All stones are equal in the eyes of this designer and all merit the same careful consideration in their presentation. Created at her bench in this lovely shop-studio, pieces incorporate the full spectrum of precious and semi-precious stones bound in gold and silver and incorporate motifs from nature as recurrent themes. She works to commission and the items on display are ideal starting points for a bespoke process that will culminate in something entirely unique. More accessible items by her can by enjoyed for as little as £25 or less for those of other British designers such as Galibardy, frillybylily and Stolen Thunder whose hand-drawn graphics wrought in wood and acrylic stand out. **Branch on the Park** is a browser's delight with portraits, paintings and a collection of crystals and fossils sure to fascinate young visitors. *GT*

MAP 6 Ref. 80
Branch on the Park
227 Victoria Park Road
Victoria Village E9 7HD
+44 (0)20 8533 7977
www.branchonthepark.co.uk
Wed–Sat 10–6pm
Sun 11–5pm

Haus is a stately parkside emporium where you'll find a sharp edit of the most stylish international design with British manufacture taking pride of place. Underpinned by heavyweights B&B Italia, Edra and Marimekko the bias favours less widely represented companies such as Lightyears (who brought you the Caravaggio lamp), Swedese and Hackney's hottest Decode, Uniformwares and Frank. Owner Andrew Tye has been working out of Hackney for over 15 years designing and making furniture under his own name. The relationships that have been forged in that time explain why you'll often find prototypes from other designers here before they hit the mainstream, making visits so rewarding. And it's hard to leave empty-handed when the smaller gift size items include such ingenious solutions as universal lids to transform old jam jars into cutting edge condiment vessels. Bespoke pieces can always be commissioned or sourced by Andrew – so do ask! *GT*

MAP 6 Ref. 75

Haus

39 Morpeth Road

Victoria Village E9 7LD

+44 (0)20 7536 9291

www.hauslondon.com

Sat 11–6pm

Sun 11–4pm

-10%

Offer ends 1st Nov 2012*

You couldn't find a better place to loaf than **Loafing**. Where, gratifyingly, you can also buy a loaf: fresh bread arrives daily from St. John's and Flour Power. Coffee is the best on the block, as voted by the Victoria Park Traders' Association last year and is served in the prettiest china you'll have sipped from in a long time. This café is a whole wonderful world away from what we've become accustomed to on the high street. The décor is alluring, owing to its previous incarnation as an antiques shop and it hasn't lost a crumb of style since. If you can drag yourself away from the sweetest piles of patisserie out front, be sure to make time for a lunchtime sarnie in the garden – Ginger Pig ham and chutney perhaps – or bag an armchair by the window for an afternoon Earl Grey with a friend. *GT*

MAP 6 Ref. 77

Loafing
79 Lauriston Road
Victoria Village E9 7MJ
+44 (0)20 8986 0777
www.loafing.co.uk
Mon–Fri 7.30–6pm
Sat 8–6pm
Sun 9–6pm

Victoria Village . *Café*

A renowned commentator of the London art scene described **The Residence** as "the place to be seen… the Guggenheim of the East End". Ever-evolving it now boasts its own guest suite for hire: an extrapolation of the enduring residential theme – home as gallery – as explored in previous incarnations at other venues. Arch directrice Ingrid Z has been curating shows since her own art school days in Canada and has her finger in the pulsing flow. If you fancy edging so close to bleeding, this is where it's at. She believes artists represent the gallery not the other way around and at The Residence she facilitates a lively roster of them: emerging and established. Prices for the freshest of 21st Century Fine Art are on a scale of affordable to serious. Underestimate at your peril. *GT*

MAP 6 Ref. 81

The Residence

229 Victoria Park Road

Victoria Village E9 7HD

+44 (0)20 8985 0321

www.residence-gallery.com

Wed–Sat 11–6pm

Sun 12–5pm

Sublime's success is built on long-standing attention to its customers needs. Starting out over a decade ago as little more than a gift shop it's been a natural evolution to its current one-stop-shop position for presents and party dresses as well as casuals for the style-savvy but time-poor mums of the East. In the cavernous vintage section downstairs however, this boutique shows its heart. A perusal uncovers not just well-chosen retro garments, shoes and accessories but some brand spanking new garb, often still bearing original tags, no doubt via way of a shoot with one of the many stylists who live nearby. There are pieces for all ages, reflecting the influence of both staff and customers. Back upstairs, labels such as ethical Peopletree and local designers emilyandfin fit well with the holistic sense of this outlet whose focus is firmly on enduring style rather than disposable fashion. A newer Clerkenwell branch continues the theme. *GT*

MAP 6 Ref. 79

Sublime
225 Victoria Park Road
Victoria Village E9 7HD
+44 (0)20 8986 7243
www.sublimeshop.co.uk
Mon–Fri 10–6pm
Sat 9–7pm
Sun 11–5pm

Victoria Village . *Fashion*

A playground that caters to children without ignoring their grown-up chums, **The Toybox** is tardis-like in its scope, packed to the rafters with fun stuff, most items priced comfortably under £20. There's a play area for youngsters and a music policy to cheer adult ears. With years of experience in other toyshops and a commitment to civic participation, French owner Loic so impressed neighbouring businesses that he was able to finance the new shop from within the community. His tribute to the area is an array of imaginative and well-made games and toys dominated by the gorgeous French range Djeco whose crafty kits and removable sticker sets are deserved top-sellers alongside Sockette puppets (for long arms as much as little fingers) packed in amongst all the old favourites: board games, marbles, trainsets, puzzles, books and, as you might expect from a French proprietor, some particularly chic clothing. *GT*

MAP 6 Ref. 78
The Toybox
223 Victoria Park Road
Victoria Village E9 7HD
+44 (0)20 8533 2879
www.thetoyboxshop.co.uk
Mon–Sun 9–6pm

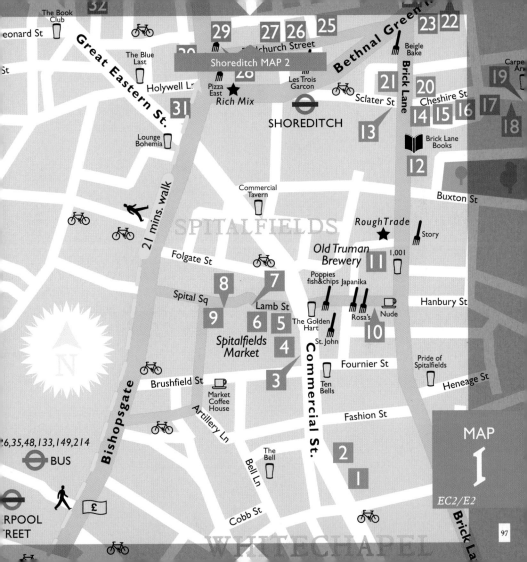

The Book Club

Great Eastern St.

Leonard St

St

The Blue Last

Holywell Ln

32

30

Pizza East

Rich Mix

★

29

Shoreditch MAP 2

27 **26** **25**

Bethnal Green R.

23 **22**

Beigle Bake

Fulchurch Street

28

Les Trois Garcon

21

Brick Lane

Sclater St

20

Cheshire St

19

Carpe Arr

31

Lounge Bohemia

SHOREDITCH

13

14 **15** **16**

17

18

Brick Lane Books

12

Commercial Tavern

Buxton St

SPITALFIELDS

21 mins. walk

RoughTrade ★

Story

Old Truman Brewery **11**

1,001

Folgate St

Spital Sq

8

7

Poppies fish&chips Japanika

Hanbury St

Lamb St

9

6 **5**

The Golden Hart

Rosa's

Nude

Spitalfields Market

4

St. John

10

3

Fournier St

Pride of Spitalfields

Heneage St

Brushfield St

Market Coffee House

Ten Bells

Commercial St.

Fashion St

Artillery Ln

MAP

1

6,35,48,133,149,214

BUS

Bell Ln

The Bell

2

I

EC2/E2

RPOOL REET

£

Cobb St

Brick La

WHITECHAPEL

97

N

Bishopsgate

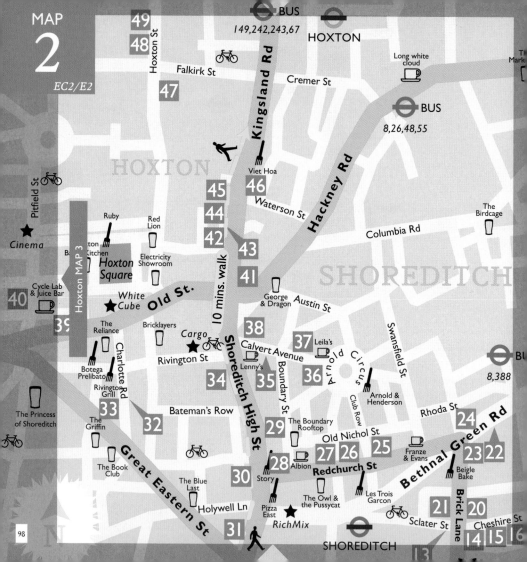

MAP
2

EC2/E2

BUS
149,242,243,67
HOXTON

Long white
cloud

BUS
8,26,48,55

49
48
Hoxton St

Falkirk St

Kingsland Rd

Cremer St

47

HOXTON

Viet Hoa

45
44
42

46

Waterson St

Hackney Rd

Columbia Rd

The
Birdcage

43

41

SHOREDITCH

Ruby

Red
Lion

...ton
Kitchen

Hoxton
Square

Electricity
Showroom

George
& Dragon

Austin St

Hoxton MAP 3

Cinema

Pitfield St

40

39

Cycle Lab
& Juice Bar

White
Cube

Old St.

The
Reliance

Bricklayers

Cargo

Rivington St

Swansfield St

38

37 Leila's

Calvert Avenue

Lenny's

36

Arnold Circus

Arnold &
Henderson

Botega
Prelibato

Rivington
Grill

33

34

35

Boundary St

Charlotte Rd

Shoreditch High St

Bateman's Row

32

Club Row

Rhoda St

24

The Princess
of Shoredith

The
Griffin

29

The Boundary
Rooftop

Old Nichol St

25

Franze
& Evans

Bethnal Green Rd

23 22

Great Eastern St

The Book
Club

The Blue
Last

30

28

Albion

Story

27 26

Les Trois
Garcon

Beigle
Bake

Redchurch St

Holywell Ln

31

Pizza
East

RichMix

The Owl &
the Pussycat

21

Sclater St

20

Brick Lane

Cheshire St

14 15 16

N

SHOREDITCH

13

The
Mark...

BU...

8,388

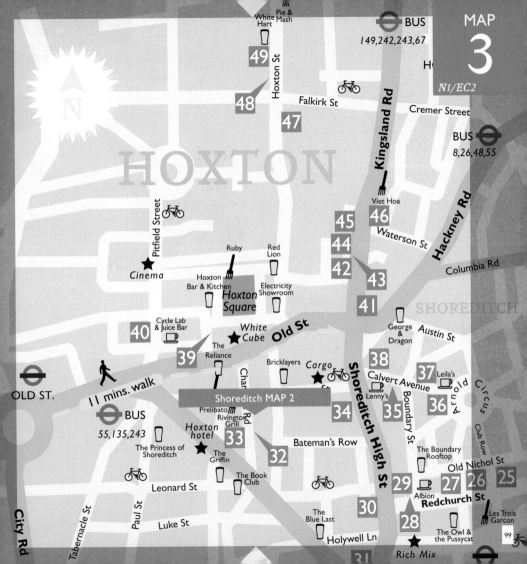

MAP
3

N1/EC2

HOXTON

SHOREDITCH

White Hart 49

Pie & Mash

Hoxton St

48

Falkirk St

47

BUS
149,242,243,67

Kingsland Rd

Cremer Street

BUS
8,26,48,55

Hackney Rd

Viet Hoa 46

Waterson St

Columbia Rd

45

44

42

43

41

Pitfield Street

Ruby

Red Lion

Cinema

Hoxton Bar & Kitchen

Hoxton Square

Electricity Showroom

George & Dragon

Austin St

40

Cycle Lab & Juice Bar

White Cube

Old St

39

The Reliance

Bricklayers

Cargo

Shoreditch High St

38

37 Leila's

Calvert Avenue

Lenny's

36

Arnold

Circus

Club Row

OLD ST.

11 mins. walk

Shoreditch MAP 2

34

35

Boundary St

BUS
55,135,243

Prelibato

Rivington Grill

Hoxton hotel

33

Bateman's Row

The Princess of Shoreditch

The Griffin

The Book Club

32

The Boundary Rooftop

29

Albion

27

Old Nichol St

26

25

Redchurch St

Leonard St

30

Paul St

Luke St

The Blue Last

Holywell Ln

28

The Owl & the Pussycat

Les Trois Garcon

99

Tabernacle St

City Rd

Rich Mix

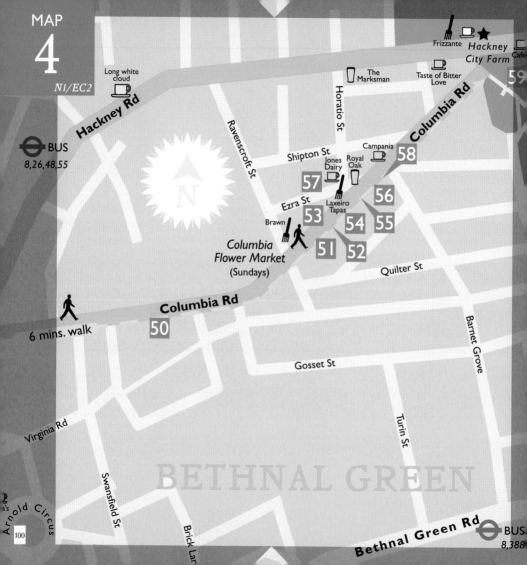

MAP
4
N1/EC2

Frizzante

Hackney City Farm

Cafe

59

Long white cloud

The Marksman

Taste of Bitter Love

Hackney Rd

Columbia Rd

Ravenscroft St

Horatio St

BUS
8,26,48,55

N

Shipton St

Campania

Jones Dairy

Royal Oak

57

58

Ezra St

56

Laxeiro Tapas

53

54

55

Brawn

Columbia Flower Market
(Sundays)

51

52

Quilter St

Columbia Rd

6 mins. walk

50

Gosset St

Barnet Grove

Virginia Rd

Turin St

BETHNAL GREEN

Arnold Circus

100

Swansfield St

Brick Lar

Bethnal Green Rd

BUS
8,388

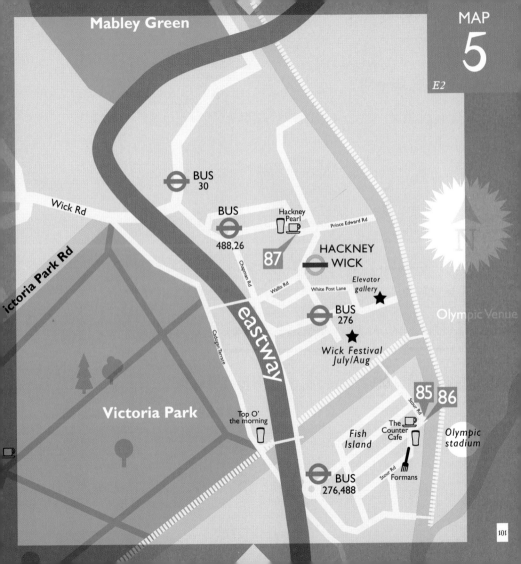

MAP
5

E2

Mabley Green

Wick Rd

ictoria Park Rd

BUS
30

BUS
488,26

Hackney
Pearl

Prince Edward Rd

87

HACKNEY
WICK

Elevator
gallery

Chapman Rd

Wallis Rd

White Post Lane

BUS
276

Wick Festival
July/Aug

Cadogan Terrace

eastway

Olympic Venue

Victoria Park

Top O'
the morning

85 86

Stour Rd

The
Counter
Cafe

Olympic
stadium

Fish
Island

Stour Rd

Formans

BUS
276,488

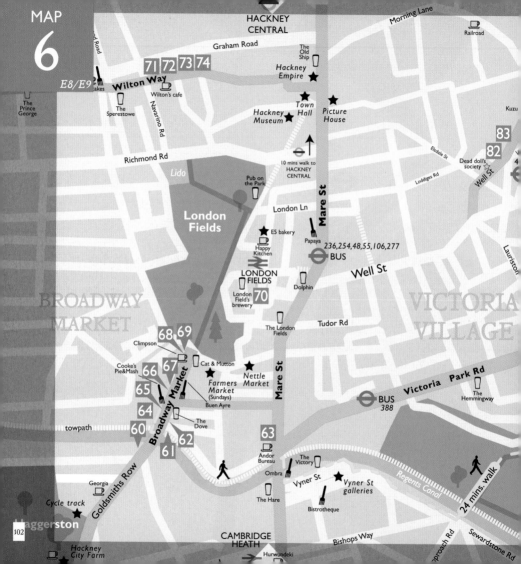

MAP
6

E8/E9

HACKNEY CENTRAL

Morning Lane

Railroad

Graham Road

The Old Ship

Hackney Empire

71 72 73 74

Wilton Way

Wilton's cafe

The Sperestowe

Navarino Rd

The Prince George

Richmond Rd

Lido

London Fields

Hackney Museum

Town Hall

Picture House

Kuzu

Elsdale St

Dead doll's society

Well St

83

82

Loddiges Rd

10 mins walk to HACKNEY CENTRAL

Pub on the Park

London Ln

Mare St

E5 bakery

Happy Kitchen

Papaya

236,254,48,55,106,277
BUS

Well St

LONDON FIELDS

London Field's brewery

70

Dolphin

BROADWAY MARKET

VICTORIA VILLAGE

The London Fields

Tudor Rd

68 69

Climpson

Cat & Mutton

Cooke's Pie&Mash

67

66

Farmers Market (Sundays)

Nettle Market

Mare St

Victoria Park Rd

BUS

The Hemmingway

65

Buen Ayre

64

60

towpath

Broadway Market

The Dove

62

61

63

Andor Bureau

Ombra

388

The Victory

Vyner St galleries

Regents Canal

24 mins. walk

Georgia

Cycle track

Haggerston

The Hare

Vyner St

Bistrotheque

Approach Rd

Sewardstone Rd

Hackney City Farm

CAMBRIDGE HEATH

Hurwundeki

Bishops Way

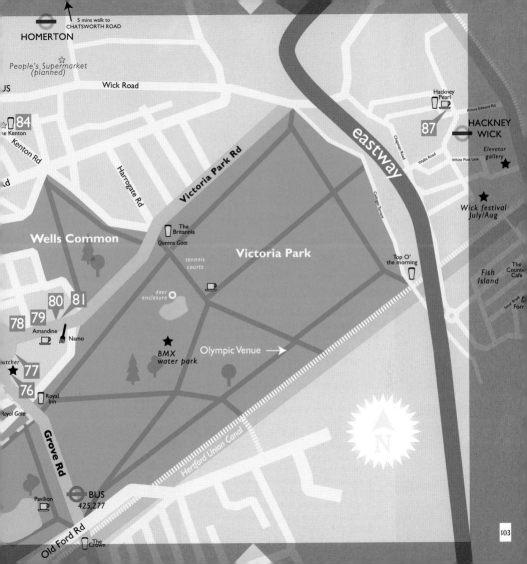

HOMERTON

5 mins walk to
CHATSWORTH ROAD

People's Supermarket
(planned)

Wick Road

Hackney
Pearl

Prince Edward Rd

84

The Kenton

87

HACKNEY
WICK

Kenton Rd

Elevator
gallery

White Post Lane

Harrogate Rd

Victoria Park Rd

Chapman Road

eastway

Wallis Road

Wick festival
July/Aug

Wells Common

The
Britannia

Queens Gate

Victoria Park

Cadogan Terrace

tennis
courts

Top O'
morning

Fish
Island

The
Count
Cafe

deer
enclosure

Stour Road

Forr

80 81

78 79

Amandine

Namo

BMX
water park

Olympic Venue →

utcher

77

76

Royal
Inn

Royal Gate

Grove Rd

Hertford Union Canal

N

Pavilion

BUS
425,277

Old Ford Rd

The
Crown

103

Locals often dodge **Central London**, but with just a little effort it can reveal a wealth of rewards. For one, it's the culinary heart of the city, eternally making space for yet more world-class restaurants – most recently, Ottolenghi's mew venture Nopi, tapas heaven The Riding House Café and Polpo's sibling, Spuntino, have all made their mark. Drinkers, meanwhile, can revel in Two Floors, which offers a taste of East End nightlife within striking distance of Carnaby Street; and The Social (off Regent Street) – one of the capital's best boutique clubs, with a snug bar on street level as well as a basement dancefloor manned by in-the-know promoters. The centre also makes room for world-class galleries, from the iconic Royal Academy and ICA to the wonderful Haunch of Venison with its endlessly intriguing programme of international contemporary art.

WC1 *Lamb's Conduit Street*

WC2 *Covent Garden*

WC2 *Seven Dials*

W1 *Soho*

W2 *Carnaby*

W2 *Connaught Village*

W2 *Portman Square*

W1 *Bloomsbury*

SW1 *Belgravia*

SW1 *Pimlico*

CENTRAL

Ben Pentreath

There is something so familiar about **Ben Pentreath**, perhaps it's the nostalgic paintings of the English countryside by wartime artist Eric Ravillious or the curious sideboard dishes made from old stamps set in resin. An interior architect by trade, Ben set up shop selling beautiful and interesting things that inspired him. Working in close collaboration with Bridie who introduces her love of curiosities to the shop, they have created a den of English treasures, including a large selection of plaster mouldings cast from a personal collection of antiques. Victorian domes and glassware in bright sapphire and ruby colours interspersed with eclectic and elegant modern table lamps by Mariana Kennedy who combines bookcloth lampshades with almost fluorescent resin bases. Giant log baskets made from woven rattan flank the entrance where geological survey maps of England and Wales feature alongside traditional kitchenware, shovels, feather dusters and heavy glass tumblers and sherry glasses sit atop antique furniture. *PB*

MAP 7 Ref. 3
Ben Pentreath Ltd
17 Rugby Street
Bloomsbury WC1N 3QT
+44 (0)20 7430 2526
www.benpetreath.com
Mon–Sat 11–6pm

Some might say it's a pretty bold move painting a shop black and white, however, I doubt any would argue that it's certainly an effective way to showcase the sculptural wares they have on display. Essentially selling accessories, whether for fashion or the home, **Darkroom** explores materials and their uses, selling soft leather bags with a fine wood trim or wall hangings made of heavy wool appearing like oversized pieces of jewellery. With backgrounds in fashion and interiors a lot of time goes into curating the store with the theme changing seasonally and in conjunction with the designers they work with, many of whom draw inspiration from Africa in a modernist way. Monochrome paintings line the wall evoking illusions of black mirrors and solid black plinths off-set against a geometric patterned floor display covetable gold and silver jewellery, and tribal themed accessories mixed with woven leather belts and conspicuous homewares. *PB*

MAP 7 Ref. 2

Darkroom
52 Lamb's Conduit Street
Bloomsbury WC1N 3LL
+44 (0)20 7831 7244
www.darkroomlondon.com
Mon–Fri 11–7pm
Sat 11–6pm

Bloomsbury . Home

-10%

Discount*

Francophiles will adore this retail homage to all things French. Not only is the stock an eclectic mix of French-style textiles, toiletries, kitchenware, vintage lighting and even artisan children's toys, but **The French House** boutique itself has a rustic continental look, with antique tables and dressers and a backroom decked out like a French farmhouse kitchen. The emphasis is on products sourced from small manufacturers and artisan producers and, while not everything is actually from France, every effort is made to order only beautiful, quality items from across Europe that have a distinct French feel. Expect stunning quilts and linens made by a family firm in Paris, traditional pottered stoneware from Cher, intoxicating perfumes and pretty hand-finished scented candles. *ZA*

MAP 7 Ref. 1
The French House
50 Lamb's Conduit Street
Bloomsbury WC1N 3LJ
+44 (0)20 7831 1111
www.thefrenchhouse.net
Mon–Fri 11–7pm
Sat 11–6pm

It was on a trip to the south of France some while back that **Maggie Owen** came across a beautiful beaded necklace. It was with this necklace and its unusual sculptural quality that she was inspired to open her own shop in this unique former dairy. Although her main focus is on costume jewellery primarily from renowned Parisian designer Philippe Ferrandis, her love of sculpture and anything jewel-like is evident throughout the store. Unusual beaded animals from a womens' collective in Cape Town are mixed with ethnic and regal semi-precious necklaces, earrings and bracelets in ethereal colours and fantastical designs. A striking silk piece from textile designer Margot Selby adorns the wall and fanciful balsa wood sculptures of the Eiffel tower from a Chinese supermarket in Madrid are intermittently placed amongst Faber and Faber books with beautiful covers and stacks of fashion magazines. *PB*

MAP 7 Ref. 4

Maggie Owen
13 Rugby Street
Bloomsbury WC1N 3QT
+44 (0)20 7404 7070
www.maggieowenlondon.com
Mon–Sat 11–6pm

Like walking into a kaleidoscope **Margo Selby** is a blast of striking colour and geometric pattern. Brightly coloured cashmere scarves and silk fabrics with designs so textured they look three-dimensional and colours so vivid they are virtually fluorescent. A well established weaver Margo describes herself as a craftswoman first and a business woman second believing that handwoven qualities are too special to let die out. All the products sold in the store, from bedspreads to purses, buttons and ties are made in the atelier in the basement where the handloom is constantly whirring. Margo treats rugs and textiles like paintings, adoringly putting colours together creating theatrical and luxurious designs with books of sensational fabric swatches where customers can take their pick from various silks and upholstery fabrics. And it doesn't stop there; fun gift cards, coasters, mugs and plates emblazoned with the famous London landmark Trellik Tower complete the collection. *PB*

MAP 7 Ref. 7

Margo Selby
4–11 Galen Place
Pied Bull Yard
Bloomsbury WC1A 2JR
+44 (0)20 7242 6322
www.margoselby.com
Mon–Sat 10–6pm

From time to time we are all faced with the inevitable problem, "What present should I get? I have to get *something…*". An apt name as '**Something**' will certainly have a suitable present for every occasion. A truly girly gift shop you will find some kind of charming object for every room of the house. Whether it's cookery books, enamel tins for the kitchen, Venetian glass mirrors and pretty tealight holders for the living room, delicious scented candles for the bedroom, or retro gardening tools for the girl with a new hobby, you won't fail. Like a mini department store of gifts you will find everything from inspired greetings cards made from old vintage playing cards to world map printed wrapping paper. The choice appears endless, including soft leather purses, picture frames, body products, children's clothes and toys and eclectic jewellery, says owner Toni, "I just don't know when to stop buying things". *PB*

MAP 7 Ref. 5

Something
58 Lamb's Conduit Street
Bloomsbury WC1N 3LW
+44 (0)20 7430 1516
www.something-shop.com
Mon–Fri 10.30–6pm
Sat 11–5pm
Open on Sun in Dec

If you've ever found yourself enjoying the gift shop more than the exhibition, **Volte Face** could be for you. Channeling the look and feel of a contemporary gallery shop, the diminutive boutique pulls together a discerning selection of products from established and emerging designers as well as arty books and cool stationery. The eclectic mix is largely down to Volte Face's two founders – Bill Godber (owner of publishing distributor Turnaround) and designer Kit Grover – and unique items betray their leftfield ethos and eye for intriguing, functional and beautiful objects. Look out for products such as the Palomar Crumpled City Map series or a Gilbert & George push-up toy among more familiar merchandise including diaries by Moleskine, bookmarks by Emotion Gallery and playful kitchenware by Seletti. *PB*

MAP 7 Ref. 6

Volte Face
21 Great Ormond Street
Bloomsbury WC1N 3JB
+44 (0)20 7430 0021
www.volteface.co.uk
Mon–Sat 10.30–6.30pm

Discount*

Inspired as a child by her mother's collection of beautiful jewellery, **Laura Lee Jewellery** designs whimsical and striking pieces influenced by stories and familiar everyday things, such as delicate necklaces, lockets and bracelets complete with intricate little star sign symbols lucky charms and old coins which make lovely pieces for everyday wear, all made in solid silver. Alongside her more playful work she creates more valuable jewellery using 18ct gold in white, yellow and rose using precious stones such as diamonds and rubies. She produces ethereal creations by using more unusual stones such as grey opals with a pretty iridescent sheen and tourmaline, popular due to the range of colours it appears in. Additionally they do bespoke work and will happily make changes to any individual pieces to ensure the wearer will be happy. *PB*

MAP 8 Ref. 21

Laura Lee Jewellery
42 Monmouth Street
Seven Dials WC2H 9EP
+44 (0)20 7379 9050
www.lauraleejewellery.com
Mon–Fri 10–6pm
Thurs 10–7pm
Sat 11–6pm
Sun 12–5pm

Free engraving on any of our solid gold items*

Mint is a breed of vintage shop that can actually call itself a vintage shop rather than just second hand, they don't buy in bags of clothes by weight here, everything is hand selected and whether it's an early 1980's denim jacket or a late 1980's one matters a great deal. A well-edited collection, they sift through hundreds of pieces to get to the perfect fifty. By closely following catwalk and street trends, suppliers are contacted in order to claim everything they predict will come into fashion. Garments must be in near-perfect condition and original, meaning Hawaiian shirts must be made in Hawaii with no missing buttons, no stains and no tears, so you will be buying as good as new. Leather jackets, thick wool jumpers, Swiss army backpacks, blazers and ankle boots are in abundance as; "sometimes we do a mass of one thing to show a bit of commitment". *PB*

MAP 8 Ref. 20

Mint
20 Earlham Street
Seven Dials WC2H 9LN
+44 (0)20 7836 3440
www.mintvintage.co.uk
Mon–Wed 11–7pm
Thu–Sat 11–8pm
Sun 12–6pm

Super Superficial is about two things; a love of t-shirts and a love of artists. Shelves lined with immaculately folded sweatshirts, hoodies and t-shirts, emblazoned with exciting street art inspired illustrations, photographs and artworks from the likes of Chris Dent and Will Thompson, all just as worthy to be framed as worn, create a mutually beneficial environment for fashion and art to co-exist. This way artists get more exposure as each garment becomes a talking piece. A straightforward idea, each t-shirt design is by a different artist with new releases each month keeping the collection current and inspired. Downstairs they have a bright art space showcasing established artists next to emerging artists, "the idea being that they are mentioned in the same sentence" creating a great platform for graduates to showcase their work and gain recognition. *PB*

MAP 8 Ref. 19

Super Superficial
22 Earlham Street
Seven Dials WC2H 9LN
+44 (0)20 7287 7447
www.supersuperficial.com
Mon–Sat 11–7pm
Sun 12–5pm

Seven Dials . *Fashion*

115

If you were to have a root through the jewellery collection of any stylish London girl, chances are you will come across at least one piece by **Tatty Devine.** Creators of witty and fun Perspex pieces, Tatty Devine are well known in fashionable circles for their quirky necklaces, earrings and bracelets. Here you will find beautifully crafted jewellery such as mirrored angel wing and heart-shaped lollipop necklaces next to crown and bow shaped rings. Keen to be involved in other creative endeavours,

Tatty Devine have done various commissioned projects creating unique and collectable pieces in collaboration with other artists such as gin bottle shaped pendants for a Gilbert and George travelling show and a Roller-skate pendant as they are the proud sponsors of the 'London Rollergirls'. The collection is complemented by a selection of girly 50's shoes and hats by the likes of Swedish brand Minimarket. *PB*

MAP 8 Ref. 22
Tatty Devine
44 Monmouth Street
Seven Dials WC2H 9EP
+44 (0)20 7836 2685
www.tattydivine.com
Mon–Sat 11–7pm
Sun 12–5pm
Late night Thu until 8pm

Where should you go if you're a busy person who needs to be comfortable and stylish from when you get dressed in the morning to cocktails at the end of the day? **Unconditional** that's where. Experts in creating rock chic pieces for both men and women using subtle colours and flattering drapery in super soft fabrics, they make dressing look effortless. With an unfussy androgynous aesthetic, which accommodates most body shapes, this is sophisticated dressing to a T. Although the shop features mainly

their own label they also stock a witty range by JC de Castelbajac with bags, shoes, shirts and knitwear emblazoned with Bambi and characters from Southpark. Additionally they also have a great range of jewellery with giant glitzy diamante gems and pale pink skulls on fine silver chains. An offbeat store with various curiosities including taxidermy rabbit heads with antlers it's a fantastic shop for those who like to reside in distinguished comfort. *PB*

MAP 8 Ref. 18

Unconditional
16 Monmouth Street
Seven Dials WC2H 9DD
+44 (0)20 7836 6931
www.unconditional.uk.com
Mon–Sat 11–7pm
Sun 12–6pm
Late night Thu until 8pm

'Hospital furniture' is what the public called the modern furniture from Le Corbusier, Castiglioni and Le Breuer, Zeev Aram had put on display in his tiny King's Road showroom. That was circa 1964. Almost fifty years later, **Aram Store** is now considered a design guru, the one who introduced along with Terence Conran of Habitat the idea of decorating your house with something else other than chintz. Since then, he may have expanded to bigger premises, like this 5-storey converted warehouse in Covent Garden. But he hasn't lost any of his insatiable passion for modern design, and along with his children, Ruth and Daniel, has never ceased to stock some of the biggest names in design. There may be some hefty price tags involved, yet the best thing is that you can just wander around in the shop's beautifully curated showroom. You can't put a price on that, for sure! *DG*

MAP 8 Ref. 27

Aram Store
110 Drury Lane
Covent Garden WC2B 5SG
+44 (0)20 7557 7557
www.aram.co.uk
Mon–Sat 10–6pm
Late night Thu until 7pm

You would be hard pressed to find a store where the customers can be overheard exclaiming "Hey that's cool!" quite so often. **Do** specialise in quirky and imaginative products like milk cartons and egg boxes cast in ceramic, alongside Japanese Bento boxes and unusual furniture such as inflatable sofas. Working with both well established and new designers each one of their products combines four features; beauty, functionality, simplicity and uniqueness (at least where possible), a mantra that serves them well. Inspired by young talent the 'do Masters', a program was started where recent graduates are given the opportunity to showcase their work in the store as long as it combines the four features of the 'do' ideal and is economically viable. With everything here, form and function go hand-in-hand. *PB*

MAP 8 Ref. 28
Do
34 Shorts Gardens
Covent Garden WC2H 9PX
+44 (0)20 7836 4039
www.do-shop.com
Mon–Wed Fri–Sat 10–6.30pm
Thu 10–8pm
Sun 12–6pm

Discount*

It's great when someone fills a gap in the market isn't it! This can be said for **Laird London**, suppliers of expertly made traditional hats of every different variety; from Baker boy, Flat-cap and Pork pie to Top Hat, Panama, Trilby and Sherlock Holmes. Established due to a love of hats and the lack of quality men's headwear, Laird realised the importance of opening a shop dedicated to the one fashion item which "completes an outfit, hats are a bold statement, they can completely change a look". Until Laird opened up, good quality hats were hard to come by, everything was either very dull or very expensive. With a good cross section of classic hats of exceptional quality, they do limited runs and on different occasions produce each type of hat in different fabrics for those with a penchant for a particular style. *PB*

MAP 8 Ref. 25

Laird London

23 New Row

Covent Garden WC2N 4LA

+44 (0)20 7240 4240

www.lairdlondon.co.uk

Mon–Sat 11–7pm

Sun 12–6pm

Thanks to the latest 50s revival, geek glasses are back in fashion. But if you want to go one step beyond the current trend, Seamus **McClintock** is the guy for you. Having worked for over sixteen years in the eyewear industry (in design and retail respectively), McClintock has created a shrine to the 'bespectacled look' with his eponymous and original 'McClintock' boutique. Expect some amazing optical frames from unique designers: wooden styles by Made, colourful and modern frames by Kirk Originals or Kilsgaard, and even 50s-inspired styles by Patty Paillette. Whether you want a cool Buddy Holly look or even something inspired by Bauhaus architecture, here you will be spoilt for choice. Even though the shop stocks a huge variety of different styles, what they all have in common is the fact that they are unique, innovative and handmade. The same principle applies to sunglasses. For your eyes only. *DG*

MAP 8 Ref. 26

McClintock Eyewear
29 Floral Street
Covent Garden WC2E 9DP
+44 (0)20 7240 5055
www.mcclintock-eyewear.co.uk
Mon–Sat 11–7pm
Sun 12–5pm

Orbital Comics

Comic book shops can be intimidating and probably not the first stop on the list for those who don't wear an anorak. However, **Orbital Comics** has a totally different ambience than most comic shops as it feels more like a hang-out than a corporate merchandising machine; somewhere even those with a mild interest can pick up tips even if it's just for a love of the artwork alone. As the biggest stockist of vintage comics, Orbital has all the big name classics from Marvel and DC to a great selection of Indie and Manga along with hard to find back-issues and graphic novels. Continuing their homely feel is the homemade comics rack where people can create and sell their own titles at low prices, a nice alternative to the mainstream books. With a large gallery space, Orbital regularly hosts signings and events giving an opportunity to pick up a piece of comic history. *PB*

MAP 8 Ref. 23

Orbital Comics
8 Great Newport Street
Covent Garden WC2H 7JA
+44 (0)20 7240 0591
www.orbitalcomics.com
Mon–Sat 10.30–7pm
Sun 11.30–5pm

You have to love the fact that there is a place in London to buy 'cut out pets', yes that is an actual thing. **Tenderproduct** hosts a carefully selected collection of quirky designs, Russian doll shaped USB sticks, key chains handmade out of worn down coloured pencils and Japanese hand-stitched soft toys using re-claimed fabric so no two are the same, accompanied by their own personal story. The product shop grew from the gallery two doors down which focuses on giving young artists their first solo show. Having featured several artists who worked in miniature, the idea came about to open a shop where designers could create affordable products and explore ideas. They feature a few mass produced items all of which however, credit the designer, keeping with their independent theme. Additionally they have a small gallery space downstairs tying in the pure artistic element. *PB*

MAP 8 Ref. 24

Tenderproduct
6 Cecil Court
Covent Garden WC2N 4HE
+44 (0)20 7379 9464
www.tenderproduct.com
Tue–Sat 10–6pm

Discount*

'We don't serve soya milk here, we're purists!' A statement which sums up what **Fernandez & Wells** is all about, although I can assure you it was said in good humour. This stylish, uncluttered and utilitarian café with rustic wood floorboards and aluminium stools is a popular Soho spot packed from open to close and for good reason. Sandwiches, coffee and cakes. If you're looking for something along the lines of 'rare topside of beef with horseradish and rocket' or 'roast pork belly with apple sauce' then you've come to the right place. Everything is fresh and well sourced. The coffee is excellent and lovingly prepared with the option of a selection of delicious Portuguese custard tarts and homemade almond and clementine loaf. And it doesn't stop there. Around the corner they have a food and wine bar where you can indulge in a variety of expertly picked wines, cured meats, cheese and bread. *PB*

MAP 8 Ref. 16

Fernandez & Wells

43 Lexington Street

Soho W1F 9AL

+44 (0)20 7287 8124

www.fernandezandwells.com

Mon–Sun 11–11pm

For members of the Clash, the Ramones and the Sex Pistols there was only one leather jacket to be worn and that was one by **Lewis Leathers**. Established in 1892 the company made protective clothing for the increasingly popular pursuits of motoring, motorcycling and flying, going on to make outfits for the RAF during World War II. Nostalgic posters and music ornament the shop along with old leather jackets embellished with patches and badges, flying helmets and well-worn leather biker boots.

Specialising in the mid fifties to late seventies period, the shop features rails of jackets for both men and women in varying styles with names such as 'Lightening' and 'Easy Rider' and boots still manufactured from original 1967 patterns. After the war with the affluent youth movement wanting to look like Marlon Brando in the Wild One the Bronx Jacket was created being an instant hit, securing Lewis Leathers in the Rockers hall of fame. *PB*

MAP 8 Ref. 8

Lewis Leathers
3-5 Whitfield Street
Fitzrovia W1T 2SA
+44 (0)20 7636 4314
www.lewisleathers.com
Mon–Sat 11–6pm

Soho . *Fashion*

Pokit

We need to take a few steps back to a time when being properly dressed was the norm. For those who aren't prepared to take out a second mortgage, **Pokit** specialise in affordable, casual, tailor-made suits. Adhering to a very British aesthetic using a range of good quality tweeds, corduroy, wool flannel and cotton twill they follow time-honoured British tailoring techniques where service is the same for both men and women. With no need for an appointment, you can just walk in off the street and take your pick from a selection of tailored trousers in all manner of colours and styles hung elegantly from copper pipes. They have a number of sample size jackets for customers to try on and an in-house stylist to advise on the fit and style of your bespoke suit, ready in two to three weeks. To complete the look see their range of leather bags, shoes and accessories. *PB*

MAP 8 Ref. 17

Pokit
132 Wardour Street
Soho W1F 8ZW
+44 (0)20 7434 2875
www.pokit.co.uk
Mon–Fri 11–7pm
Sat 11–5pm

A true hub of creativity and innovation, there are no rules at **Beyond the Valley**, just so long as it's not ordinary. Homewares are interspersed with clothes, accessories, gifts and non-sequential items, such as knitted toys and ceramic boxes in the shape of biscuits, basically anything that takes their fancy really. Playful and quirky designs are printed onto ceramic mugs, plates and notebooks and brightly coloured screen prints furnish the silver and gold papered walls. A unique space showcasing young designer talent, Beyond the Valley features the cream of the crop of London's fashion, product and jewellery designers. Alongside a selection of wearable items and printed t-shirts you will find beautifully crafted clothes that challenge functionality, shoes that look like sculptures and cabinets displaying jewellery that combines precious metals with leather, ribbon, Perspex, flocking, wood, feathers and rope. *PB*

MAP 8 Ref. 13
Beyond the Valley
2 Newburgh Street
Carnaby W1F 7RD
+44 (0)20 7437 7338
www.beyondthevalley.com
Mon–Sat 11–7pm
Sun 12.30–5pm

Soho . *Home*

It may be a while before **F-Troupe** wins that much coveted Royal Warrant. "Cobblers to her Majesty" announces the sign above the door. And so to the shoes: in keeping with everything in this contemporary curiosity shop they display a particularly British blend of eccentricity and sensible practicality. Huntin', shootin', fishin' with an urban edge, made for the pavements of a modern metropolis. Current styles include a most ladylike boot with a flexible, hard-wearing rubber foot and a Harris Tweed upper, Victorian in contour. Another comes with pin-tucked leather around heel and toe. Clearly with an eye on blue-blooded patronage F-Troupe even has Corgis. No, not the four-legged mutts that snap at your ankles but Welsh woollen socks to warm them instead. And it's all brought to you by staff from a bygone era; smart and smiling. F-Troupe, fit for a Queen. *GT*

MAP 8 Ref. 12
F Troupe
33 Marshall Street
Carnaby W1F 7ET
+44 (0)20 7494 4566
www.f-troupe.com
Mon–Sat 11–7pm

-10%
Discount*

A block north of Oxford Street there exists a parallel universe. And once enjoyed there's no going back. Eastcastle Street is typical of many in the area: barely a minute's walk away from the heave and fury of the busiest shopping street in Europe yet it remains calm, civilised and entirely underpopulated. As London's answer to New York's Garment District, it now houses many art galleries too. Nestled in the middle of all this is **Fever**. Luxuriating in space, with a favela flavour to its décor, here you'll find three distinct fashion collections, a great value sample and vintage rail (the inspiration for their lines), the best changing rooms in town, and if you're thinking "what a space for a party!", well, they got there before you. This team likes to shop in style, throwing themed events with drinks and canapes, swing bands and dancing. Get on that mailing list! *GT*

MAP 8 Ref. 9

Fever
52 Eastcastle Street
Carnaby W1W 8ED
+44 (0)20 7636 6326
www.feverdesigns.co.uk
Mon–Sat 11–7pm
Sun 12–5pm

Carnaby . **Fashion**

Fur Coat No Knickers. For a wedding? Maybe! Because anything's possible after playing dress-up in the fitting room at Laura and Emma's W1 atelier. These two ex-theatreland costume supervisors started their business supplying vintage accessories to TV and film productions only to find themselves sending period-perfect brides down the aisle. What happened? They were good! Years of experience through red-eye sewing sessions to meet crazy deadlines, all so the show could go on, gave them the edge brides appreciate for their performance of a lifetime. The duo's skill is to customise vintage stock from the 1930s-60s, ensuring it fits like a glove and looks like new. Garments are sourced from across the globe. Prom frocks, day dresses, sheaths worthy of the silver screen, all can be re-modelled to create a unique and alternative look. But whether it's old, new, borrowed or blue, remember ladies: the wearing of pants is up to you. *GT*

MAP 8 Ref. 15

Fur Coat No Knickers

Top Floor

Kingly Court

Carnaby W1B 5PW

+44 (0)7814 002 295

www.furcoatnoknickers.co.uk

Mon–Sat 11–7pm

Tues 11–5.30pm

Sun 12.30–5pm

If Joe Perry or Slash were to advise you on what guitar to buy you'd listen to them wouldn't you? Well the same can be said for Nicki Sixx and Lemmy when it comes to jewellery. If members of Motley Crue and Motorhead claim **The Great Frog** is the greatest Rock n Roll jewellery shop in London well you'd be a fool to argue. Purveyors of bespoke jewellery for the great and the good of the heavy metal scene since 1972 it was a father to son hand-over affair. Each piece is hand-finished in the basement below the shop by a team of trained artisans headed by Reino, who was trained by his father from the age of fifteen. Black antique cabinets display human skulls and Hannya masks, mixed with heavy, precious metal pieces including Rhino head rings, crucifixes and skulls hanging on bulky chains embedded with deep purple amethyst stones. *PB*

MAP 8 Ref. 14

The Great Frog
10 Ganton Street
Carnaby W1F 7QR
+44 (0)20 7439 9357
www.thegreatfroglondon.com
Mon–Sat 10.30–6.30pm
Sun 12–5pm

Carnaby . Fashion

Joy Everley

In need of a special piece of jewellery and Tiffany isn't your cup of tea? Then try one of the longest established shops on the block, **Joy Everley**. This mother and daughter duo make elegant and timeless pieces in traditional and eccentric designs using precious metals and a variety of different stones. There are hundreds of wonderfully detailed and whimsical charms to choose from including top hats, roller-skates and cowboy boots with a variety of different bracelets and necklaces. Other key elements to the collection include a more traditional range of wedding and engagement rings for those that want something simple but beautifully made and their sparkling cocktail rings and earrings will glamorize any outfit, Hollywood style. An elegant and understated shop with panelled walls, oriental rugs and chandeliers; this really is a treasure trove of jewellery with a piece suitable for every taste and occasion. *PB*

MAP 8 Ref. 11
Joy Everley
7 Newburgh Street
Carnaby W1F 7RH
+44 (0)20 7287 2792
www.joyeverley.co.uk
Mon–Sat 10.30–6.30pm
Thur late night till 8pm

Fashion . Carnaby

-10%
*Discount**

Do you like biscuits and bright colours? Bobbles, googly things and watching telly? Are you forty-going-on-fourteen? Or just fourteen? You know **Lazy Oaf** already don't you! Secretly, for years, you've been saving your take-away menus and filing them in the Take Away Menu Organiser (£8.99), keeping notes on your favourite nosh. Home-baking's been a doddle with the Glove and Cake oven mitts (£15) and you keep your gaming mates sweet with the Pacman Cookie Cutters (£12.75). Not all your friends totally

get the pizza sweatshirt but your badge collection is second to none and they were dead jealous of the hot dog scarf. It's a tough old world though and not everyone loves a potato head (birthday card £2.75): some folk are really far too serious. But when you finally plucked up the courage to write that special someone "I like you nearly as much as crisps" (card £2.75) you won a heart. *GT*

MAP 8 Ref. 10

Lazy Oaf
19 Fouberts Place
Carnaby W1F 7QE
+44 (0)20 7287 2060
www.lazyoaf.com
Mon–Sat 10.30–7pm
Thur till 8pm
Sun 12p–6pm

Carnaby . **Fashion**

133

It's like walking into a movie star's wardrobe, every couture designer worth their salt hangs on the rails of **Atelier Mayer.** The store describes itself as a gallery boutique and came about to complement the website www.atelier-mayer.com, providing a showroom and a space where customers can try on gorgeous pieces from Oscar de la Renta to Chanel. Created by Carmen Mayer the concept derives from her late grandmother, a haute couture seamstress in Vienna in 1927 and part of the Vienna Workshop, a production community of visual artists. The store itself has a simple sophistication with black lacquered furniture and handpicked beautifully restored garments. Downstairs they have a more exclusive luxury vintage salon frequently lending to stars for red carpet events, as they know how to do glamour the proper old-fashioned way. *PB*

MAP 9 Ref. 32

Atelier Mayer

47 Kendal Street

Connaught Village W2 2BU

+44 (0)207 706 7200

www.atelier-mayer.com

Mon–Sat 10–6pm

-10%

*Discount**

With paint-splattered canvas stretched across the floor, old cabinets of curiosities and stacks of elegant fabric, not to mention shelves full of books and artistic magazines, **Clark & Reilly** is like, for one moment you've stepped back in time. Finding yourself in this theatrical setting amongst chipped furniture, worn old armchairs and a reclaimed Macdonalds restaurant sign, you might wonder what kind of shop you've walked into. Bridget Dwyer and David Grocott travel the world seeking out treasured artefacts and textiles, refurbishing them and working closely with a team of artisans to create unique and inspired pieces. Romantics at heart they fall in love with the object, where it came from and who used it rather than the specific 'look'. They love giving new life to things and reworking vintage items, whether it's a chandelier made out of Victorian jelly moulds or a hooped underskirt now a ceiling lampshade, the possibilities are endless. *PB*

MAP 9 Ref. 34
Clarke & Reilly
8 Porchester Place
Connaught Village W2 2BS
+44 (0)20 7262 3500
www.clarkandreilly.com
Tue–Sat 10–6pm

Clarke & Reilly

Cocomaya – like a scene from the movie 'Chocolat', this exquisite artisan chocolate shop brimming with colourful plates of dainty and elegant chocolates dusted in edible gold powder in unconventional flavours such as Earl Grey and lavender, certainly has a sense of humour. The creation of three fashion veterans, you have to love the irony of stands piled high with buttery pastries and delicious cakes, not to mention the rows of perfect truffles in fluorescent coloured wrappers. The adjoining café offers a delicious lunch with soup and salads from kiwi and tomato to fig, yogurt and Parma ham where they make everything from A-Z on the premises. Housed in a listed building, the rustic shelves stacked with bars of chocolate in irresistible packaging, embellished with colourful flowers and birds flecked with gold, and antique metallic pink cabinets full of vintage tea sets and Toby jugs certainly makes this the Christian Lacroix of chocolate shops. *PB*

MAP 9 Ref. 31

Cocomaya

12 Connaught Street

Connaught Village W2 2AF

+44 (0)20 7706 2770

www.cocomaya.co.uk

Mon–Fri 7–7pm

Sat 8–7pm

Sun 8–6pm

Luxury cashmere is given a contemporary twist by Tamsin de Roemer at this Connaught Village boutique. The former model-turned-designer – known for her collaboration with Jade Jagger and jewellery label Asprey & Garrard – opened the store with husband Justin Packshaw in 2010, successfully filling a gap in the cashmere market with an edgy take on the classic fabric. As well as 100 per cent cashmere cardigans, jumpers, scarves and leggings in colours that range from neutrals to neons, the collection makes room for silk cashmere designs such as a glam off the shoulder dress with Lurex. To complete the luxe look, **De Roemer** also designs and produces bespoke precious and semi-precious jewellery as well as style-focused but not trend-led leather handbags and clutches. Impressed clients include Rachel Weisz, Kate Moss and Sylvie Guillem. ZA

MAP 9 Ref. 33

De Roemer
16 Porchester Place
Connaught Village W2 2AY
+44(0)20 3463 1970
www.deroemer.com
Mon–Fri 10–6pm
Sat 11–6pm

Connaught Village . *Fashion*

137

Purveyors of luxury loungewear, **Me&Em** design clothes that feel comfy, yet look fit to be worn to a cocktail party. Was there ever a greater invention I ask you? Using a base fabric known as 'Modal' a material 50% more water-absorbent than cotton they produce heavy yet super soft garments that are ideal around the house but totally respectable to collect the kids from school. They have an extensive range of cashmere, linen and jersey and include a few tailored 100% wool jersey pieces, orchestrated towards workwear. They keep the colour range versatile and simple, sticking with earthy tones, moss green, beige, black, grey and so on. In addition to their own collection they buy in brands that complement the look including everyday t-shirts, Falke tights and pretty ballerina pumps. *PB*

MAP 9 Ref. 30

Me&Em
21 Connaught Street
Connaught Village W2 2AY
08456 800975
www.meandem.com
Mon–Sat 10–6pm
Thu late night till 8pm

It was after traipsing the streets of Paris and New York seeking out dens of iniquity, that Sara realised that what London lacked was enough one-stop fashion boutiques for clothes, accessories and other gorgeous bits and pieces to clutter up a dressing table. So with that she set up **Viola**. Here they stock a broad range of 'wardrobe solutions', wearable clothes (that can be put in the wash) for girls who like to layer, and unique pieces such as leather leggings and mad hand-printed trainers. With a background

in specialist boutiques Sara knows a thing or two about good service as well. Viola works with people who create unique and interesting things whether it's pop art signs and screen-printed t-shirts or just people with an unbridled enthusiasm for what they do. Glamorous pieces are effective accents to the shop, all to the soundtrack of crazy retro Italian music. *PB*

MAP 9 Ref. 29
Viola
25 Connaught Street
Connaught Village W2 2AY
+44 (0)20 7262 2722
www.violalondon.com
Mon–Sat 10.30–6pm

So your home or office is in need of a new look but it's important that it works around that 18th Century painting you inherited from your grandmother. Interior designer **Eliská** is a master of mixing old with new. Here you will find a grand collection of leather and antique silverware including a beautiful backgammon set, a 1900's travelling condiment case and a gentleman's crocodile skin toiletry bag complete with beaten sterling silver essentials. Her shop is a 'window' to her business, integrating her extraordinary finds, a collection of curious everyday things; candle sticks, coffee pots, toast racks all antique solid silver with a range of elegant scented candles and essential oils. Her style is aimed at a masculine audience, very black and white with splendid cowhide and patent leather topped table cloths and bespoke furniture. Nothing is off the peg and everything can be made to accommodate different desires. *PB*

MAP 9 Ref. 35

Eliská
16a New Quebec Street
Portman Square W1H 7RU
+44 (0)20 7723 5521
www.eliskadesign.com
Mon–Wed 10–6pm
Thu–Fri 11–7pm
Sat 11–5pm

Architect-turned-furniture designer Timothy Jeffery's showroom and shop is filled with beautifully designed, handcrafted furniture. The brief range succinctly demonstrates Jeffery's keen eye for timeless style and quality craftsmanship and works as an inspirational showcase for a range of traditional English hardwoods from walnut to cherry. **Timothy Mark** can talk at length about the characteristics of each wood and explain with passion the store's ethical stance on sourcing trees as well as working with specialist craftspeople. His enthusiasm is infectious and anyone with a love for artisan furniture will soon find themselves commissioning Jeffery and his designers to create a bespoke piece, be it a simple side table, or an ambitious grandfather clock. Smaller, ornamental items (think boxes, lamps and frames) by a range of established and emerging designers are also available in store. ZA

MAP 9 Ref. 36
Timothy Mark
20 New Quebec street
Portman Square W1H 7RZ
+44 (0)20 7616 9390
www.timothymark.co.uk
Mon–Sat 12–5pm

Allegra Hicks is one of those people who know about good design because all their life they have been immersed in it. To start with, she grew up in a glass house, which was designed by her Italian architect father and was fully decorated with Gio Ponti's furniture. Then she studied design in Milan and Fine Art in Brussels and soon after she started designing frescoes in London. Ultimately it was textile and fashion design that won her over, with the establishment of her eponymous label. She may have recently moved to chic Belgravia, but one thing remains constant: her truly individual, eclectic and bohemian luxe style that defines up until today her fashion and interiors brand. Here you can find beautiful kaftans, elegant tops and dresses, as well as furnishings, upholstery and even notebooks in a range of the designer's distinctive prints, like her trademark 'Drop'. *DG*

MAP 10 Ref. 40
Allegra Hicks
42 Elizabeth Street
Belgravia SW1W 9NX
+44 (0)20 7730 3275
www.allegrahicks.com
Mon–Fri 10–6pm
Sat 11–6pm

Karen Erickson and Vicki Beamon's jewellery business owes its beginnings to a shortage. While styling a runway show for another designer, they could't find the right jewellery to match the outfits, so they decided to make it themselves on the spot. Since 1983, when their eponymous label was established, the US-born duo have literally conquered the market with their trademark 'chokers' and their 'never afraid to make a statement' attitude. Big, chunky stone necklaces, floral designs, pearls, art deco pieces, bold bangles and earrings; maximalism at its best. The brand has now grown to cult status and has just recently added First Lady Michelle Obama to its loyal fan base, while it also counts in its CV collaborations with leading fashion houses. **Erickson Beamon**'s London outpost is a shrine to the duo's unique approach to jewellery design and statement pieces. One thing is for sure; you won't be able to just choose one. *DG*

MAP 10 Ref. 41

Erickson Beamon
38 Elizabeth Street
Belgravia SW1W 9NZ
+44 (0)20 7259 0202
www.ericksonbeamon.com
Mon–Fri 10–6pm
Sat 11–5pm

Howe

With an eclectic range of pieces ranging from 18th Century to modern, the shop came about quite by accident when Christopher **Howe** got sidetracked doing a restoration. As both an antique dealer and a designer he likes to find a link in the aesthetic between different pieces, finding a way of connecting them by colour, form and texture giving the shop a wonderful and esoteric appeal. Originally dealing in 18th Century furniture he now selects things that catch his eye, being more interested in the life and quality of a piece rather than which time period it's from. You will find stunning French 18th century hanging lanterns, filing cabinets from the 1930's, the odd 1960's table along with vintage Union Jack flags all of which no doubt have quite a story behind them. *PB*

MAP 10 Ref. 38

Howe

93 Pimlico Road,

Belgravia SW1W 8PH

+44 (0)20 7730 7987

www.howelondon.com

Mon–Fri 9–6pm

Sat 10.30–4.30pm

Discount*

Ever wondered what the story is behind some of the most iconic or well known perfumes out there? Ever tried to find that elusive bottle of Tabac Blond or Serge Lutens' Feminite Du Bois? Head to **Les Senteurs** in Belgravia. This small, family-run emporium is the best place for perfumes - old favourites or new independent ones. Whether you are a perfume aficionado or someone who wants something new and fresh but above all something different from the mainstream celebrity

endorsed offerings, Les Senteurs is the answer. The shop's friendly and very knowledgeable staff will take you through an olfactory experience, to help you find 'the One'. Of course if you can't make up your mind there and then, don't worry: their sample service, where you can take up to 6 mini vials back home, will enable you to choose the right potion at your own pace. *DG*

MAP 10 Ref. 39

Les Senteurs
71 Elizabeth Street
Belgravia SW1W 9PJ
+44 (0)20 7730 2322
www.lessenteurs.com
Mon–Sat 10–6pm

Belgravia. **Beauty**

Tomasz Starzewski

Fashion . Belgravia

146

Not every one can boast the late Princess Diana as one of their clients but **Tomasz Starzewski**, on the other hand, can. Not just her, but many more; from Baroness Thatcher to the model and Earl Spencer's former wife Victoria Lockwood. Starzewski has dressed them all in his unique and utterly elegant creations. Expect here a thoroughly classic and low key design sensibility for ladies of a certain kind (cocktail dresses, every day separates, eveningwear); above all expect an emphasis on superior quality. After all his mantra is «Glamour, elegance, good design, luxury'. His eponymous boutique reflects this in every sense with its minimal deco r, attention to detail and above all its commitment to friendly service. Suspended mannequins exhibit Starzewski's creations giving them a museum quality, while carefully placed blouses and separates grace the shelves. Nothing is superfluous, which is a case in point for Starzewski's discreet and timeless elegance. *DG*

MAP 10 Ref. 37

Tomasz Starzewski

97 Pimlico Road

Belgravia SW1 8PH

+44 (0)20 7730 5559

www.starzewski.com

Mon–Fri 10–6pm

Sat (By appointment only)

MAP

7

WC1

Coram's Fields
playground & park
for children

Renoir
Cinema

Bernard St

RUSSEL
SQUARE

7 min walk

Guilford St

Guilford St

Guilford St

The Lamb

Ciao
Bella

Millman St

Duke
of York

People's
☆ Supermarket

Lamb's Conduit St

Rugby St

5

Cigala

3

Perseverance

Great Ormond St

6

Queen Square

The Espresso
Room

2

4

Cockpit
Arts

The
Queens
Larder

I

Lamb's

Emerald St

£

Dombey St

Bea's of
Bloomsbury

SOUTHAMPTON ROW

Lamb's Conduit St

Harpur St

New North St

Old Gloucester St

Theobald's Rd

Red Lion St

BLOOMSBURY

ord Place

BUS
68,91,168,59,188

BUS
1,19,38,55,243,45,46

£

Cochrane
Theatre

5 mins walk to
HOLBORN

HOLBORN

7

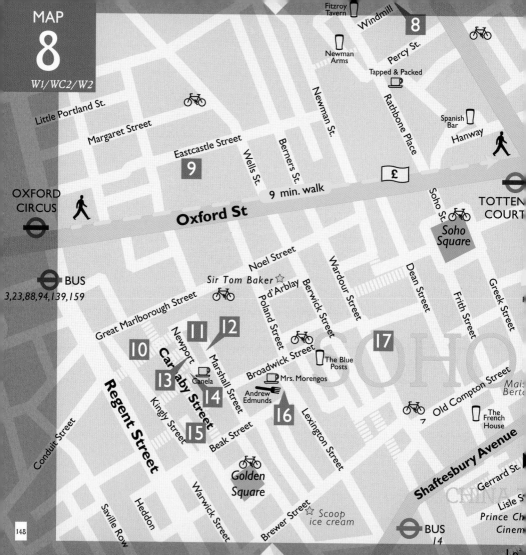

MAP
8
W1/WC2/W2

8

Fitzroy Tavern

Windmill

Newman Arms

Percy St.

Tapped & Packed

Little Portland St.

Margaret Street

Rathbone Place

Spanish Bar

Hanway

Eastcastle Street

9

Wells St.

Berners St.

Newman St.

£

OXFORD CIRCUS

9 min. walk

TOTTENHAM COURT

Oxford St

Soho St.

Soho Square

Noel Street

Wardour Street

Dean Street

Frith Street

Greek Street

BUS
3,23,88,94,139,159

Sir Tom Baker

d'Arblay

Poland Street

Berwick Street

Great Marlborough Street

Newport

11

12

17

10

Carnaby Street

13

Canela

Marshall Street

14

Broadwick Street

The Blue Posts

Mrs. Morengos

Andrew Edmunds

Old Compton Street

Mais Berto

Regent Street

Kingly Street

15

Beak Street

16

Lexington Street

The French House

SOHO

Golden Square

Conduit Street

Shaftesbury Avenue

Warwick Street

Brewer Street

Scoop ice cream

CHINA

Gerrard St.

Lisle S

Prince Ch

Cinem

Saville Row

Heddon

BUS
14

Le

BLOOMSBURY

Bloomsbury Street

Museum Tavern

British Museum

London Review

Camera Cafe

Bloomsbury Way

Cartoon Museum

Bi Won

New Oxford Street

BUS

Museum St.

BUS
1,8,19,55

HOLBORN

Kingsway

St. Giles High Street

Drury Lane

Rock & Sole

Endell Street

28

18 Monmouth

The Hospital Club

Shorts Gardens

Monmouth Street

Sarastro

Drury Lane

27

Earlham St.

Shelton Street

19

20

21

22

Long Acre

£

COVENT

GARDEN

Double Shot Coffee Co.

26

Floral Street

Opera House

Wellington St.

23

LEICESTER SQUARE

St. Martins Lane

Street

COVENT GARDEN

King

Covent Garden Piazza St.

Tavistock St.

BUS
8,9,13,15,23,91

25

Henrietta St.

Strand

24

Cecil Ct.
Antiquarian

New Row

Mas Burritos

CHARING CROSS

BUS

9,176

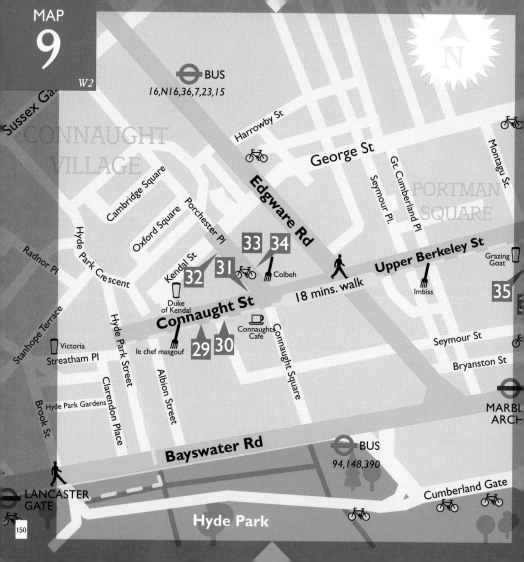

MAP
9

W2

Sussex Ga...

CONNAUGHT
VILLAGE

BUS
16,N16,36,7,23,15

Harrowby St

George St

PORTMAN
SQUARE

Montagu St.

Cambridge Square

Oxford Square

Porchester Pl

Edgware Rd

Gt. Cumberland Pl

Seymour Pl.

Hyde Park Crescent

Kendal St

33 34
Colbeh

31

32

Upper Berkeley St

Grazing
Goat

35

Radnor Pl

Duke
of Kendal

Connaught St

18 mins. walk

Imbiss

Stanhope Terrace

Victoria

Streatham Pl

le chef masgouf

29 30

Connaughts
Cafe

Connaught Square

Seymour St

Bryanston St

Hyde Park Street

Clarendon Place

Albion Street

Hyde Park Gardens

Brook St

Bayswater Rd

BUS
94,148,390

MARBL
ARCH

LANCASTER
GATE

Hyde Park

Cumberland Gate

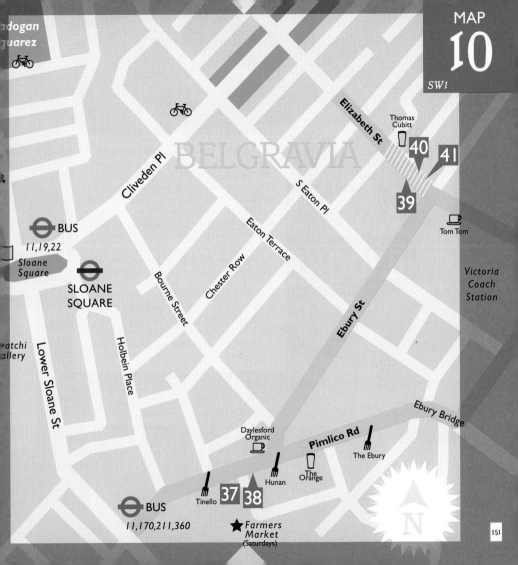

MAP

10

SW1

Cadogan
Squarez

BELGRAVIA

Elizabeth St

Thomas
Cubitt

40

41

39

Cliveden Pl

S Eaton Pl

Tom Tom

BUS
11,19,22

Eaton Terrace

Sloane
Square

Victoria
Coach
Station

SLOANE
SQUARE

Chester Row

Bourne Street

Ebury St

Saatchi
Gallery

Lower Sloane St

Holbein Place

Ebury Bridge

Daylesford
Organic

Pimlico Rd

The Ebury

The
Orange

Hunan

Tinello

37

38

BUS
11,170,211,360

★ Farmers
Market
(Saturdays)

N

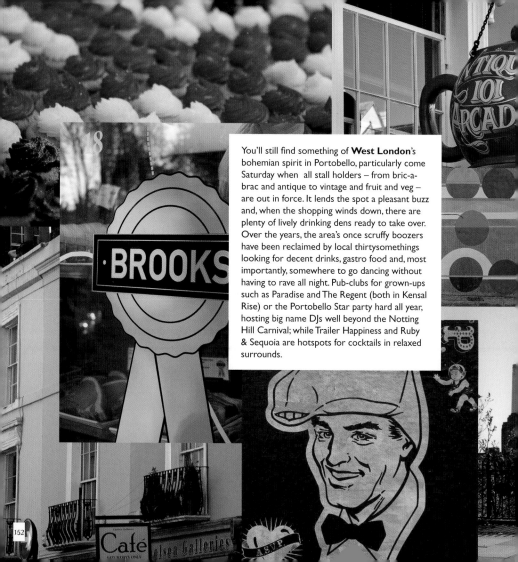

You'll still find something of **West London**'s bohemian spirit in Portobello, particularly come Saturday when all stall holders – from bric-a-brac and antique to vintage and fruit and veg – are out in force. It lends the spot a pleasant buzz and, when the shopping winds down, there are plenty of lively drinking dens ready to take over. Over the years, the area's once scruffy boozers have been reclaimed by local thirtysomethings looking for decent drinks, gastro food and, most importantly, somewhere to go dancing without having to rave all night. Pub-clubs for grown-ups such as Paradise and The Regent (both in Kensal Rise) or the Portobello Star party hard all year, hosting big name DJs well beyond the Notting Hill Carnival; while Trailer Happiness and Ruby & Sequoia are hotspots for cocktails in relaxed surrounds.

W11 *Notting Hill*
W8 *Kensington*
NW10 *Queens Park*
NW6/NW10 *Kensal Rise*
SW3 *Chelsea*
SW3 *Knightsbridge*
SW6 *Parsons Green*
SW6 *Fulham*

WEST

Ann Higgins

Anne Higgins describes her designs as 'medieval'. But don't let that fool you. What she means is wearable, vibrant, ethereal and earthy. Her knit designs have had a loyal following with writers, artists, scientists and healers for many years now due to their superior quality but also because she has also been a very well known figure in the area, having had shops on Portobello Road for over two decades. Higgins specialises in linen and wool garments, like dresses, ponchos and sweaters that are hand-knitted in workshops just outside London, using British yarns and rich silks, as well as elegant rubber macs for men and women. Her small outpost on Kensington Church Street is a testament to her creative spirit so it is no wonder her work has graced many exhibitions around Notting Hill as well as shows during the Edinburgh festival. *DG*

MAP 11 Ref. 3
Ann Higgins
107 Kensington Church Street
Notting Hill W8 7LN
+44 (0)7941 814221
Wed–Sat 11–5.30pm
and by appointment

On the outside, **Couverture & The Garbstore** may look like another cute 'Notting Hill' boutique, yet step in and you are quickly faced with a unique and thoroughly contemporary world of style that expands into three floors. Shopkeepers are Emily Dyson (daughter of James Dyson, of vacuum cleaner fame), and her husband Ian Paley (a former Paul Smith designer) and their ethos is all about offering a distinctive yet easy going view on fashion and style. A selected mix of international womenswear labels –

A Detacher, Humanoid, to name a few – is on offer, as is Paley's own menswear brand, The Garbstore, together with accessories, children's and babywear, toys, jewellery and furniture. What is great about this concept store is its relaxed attitude; you are free to wander around and try its covetable and above all affordable finds in the safe knowledge that many of the sourced items are often only available in small quantities. *DG*

MAP 12 Ref. 18

Couverture & The Garbstore
188 Kensington Park Road
Notting Hill W11 2ES
+44 (0)20 7229 2178
www.couverture.co.uk
www.garbstore.co.uk
Mon–Sat 10am–6pm
Sun (Dec only) 12–5pm

Before Shoreditch there was Notting Hill and amongst the million pound houses you can still find some of the creativity that brought the money there. Going on 15 years **The Cross** is one of the original boutiques of its kind. Opened as a pop-up shop with friends helping run it, it was one of the first places to showcase original talent, the fact that it's still here attributes to the fact that they listen to what their customers want and cater to the demands of locals after luxury and investment pieces, like pure cashmere cardigans to die for. It's all about simple, understated and comfortable clothes with a stylish twist. They have a bit of everything including a kids section and fun stationery and accessories making it a great spot for gifts too. *PB*

MAP 11 Ref. 6

The Cross
141 Portland Road
Notting Hill W11 4LR
+44 (0)20 7727 6760
www.thecrossshop.co.uk
Mon–Sat 10am–6pm

Count on Dan Lonergan to bring his classic, sleek, pared-down spirit into UK homes and offices. **Gotham**, the interiors practice and lifestyle-shop which he opened more than a decade ago is now an institution for 1930s and '40s but also contemporary American-inspired furniture (think taupe colours and the classy appeal of ebony wood) for your home or office. He also offers a unique selection of home accessories, from bespoke carpets to chinoiseries, light fittings and even artwork for sophisticated city dwellers. Lonergan,

a licenced architect himself, believes in simplifying the design process which is why his taste and services thoroughly abide by this straightforward attitude: 'Try it before you buy it'. *DG*

MAP 12 Ref. 13

Gotham
17 Chepstow Corner
1 Pembridge Villas
Notting Hill W2 4XE
+44 (0)20 7243 0011
www.gothamnottinghill.com
Mon–Fri 9–6pm
Sat 11–5pm

Notting Hill . *Home*

Pretty but with an edge to it. That is how longtime best friends and savvy mums Lucy Enfield and Sophie Worthington describe their hippy chic childrenswear line, inspired by a trip to India, called **ilovegorgeous**. Having started out six years ago out of Enfield's Notting Hill kitchen, today their shop caters for discerning young bohemian princesses, ranging from 6 months to 15 year-olds. Their style is all about vintage-inspired beautiful dresses made of precious sari Indian fabrics, good quality cottons and viscose fabrics, pretty tops, dreamy coats and cashmere cardis with subtle retro details, but all devoid of loud colours and brash logos. The ever so popular Marie Antoinette-inspired smock dress (at £106) is guaranteed to make hardcore 'tomboys' change their mind. DG

MAP 12 Ref. 14

ilovegorgeous
52 Ledbury Road
Notting Hill W11 2AJ
+44 (0)20 7229 5855
www.ilovegorgeous.co.uk
Mon–Sat 10–6pm
Sun 12–6pm

'I was a divorce lawyer and friends joked I had gone from "home-wrecker to home-maker', says Elaine Williams of her leap from the dark corridors of the court to the stylish world of interior design, in which she has been working for the past 6 years. **Interior Couture** is her design studio-cum-impromptu 'gallery' space, in which she and her design team have carefully curated a collection of pieces of furniture, from 1940's Perspex and bronze chandeliers to beautifully handcrafted sofas and chairs, vintage fabric cushions, one-off pieces from new designers from the Royal College of Art, even some objets d'art and vintage furniture, gathered from their travels and trips to antique markets. The mix is as eclectic as ever but there is a reason. As Williams says, 'my ethos is all about being practical, comfortable, pleasing; interior design shouldn't be about a finished product on your door but should grow with the client.' *DG*

MAP 12 Ref. 16

Interior Couture

118 Talbot Road London

Notting Hill W11 1JR

+44 (0)20 7792 9775

www.interiorcouture.com

Mon–Fri 10–6pm

Sat 11–5pm

Sun 12–5pm

Believe it or not, there was once a time when Notting Hill was an area you wouldn't go unless you had an armoured car, **The Jacksons** remember this time as the shop has been around for nearly fifteen years, that's saying something. It's not hard to understand why though if what you're after is good quality, comfortable yet stylish and fun everyday clothes then this is the place to come. Originally shoe designers, the Jacksons opened the shop as a way to accessorise the shoes as "it's hard to buy shoes without being able to visualise an outfit". The shop is bright and inviting with colourful scarves, beaded belts, super soft cardigans and an eclectic collection of dresses, tops, coats and trousers, you'll have everything you need to complete an outfit. *PB*

MAP 12 Ref. 17
The Jacksons
5 All saints Road
Notting Hill W11 1HA
+44 (0)20 7792 8336
www.thejacksons.co.uk
Mon–Fri 10–6pm
Sat 11–6pm

*Discount**

You have lived a bohemian life in Ibiza for ten years; your mother was a famous socialite and model turned human rights activist; Andy Warhol used to baby sit for you; your father is the lead singer of the Rolling Stones. If only **Jade Jagger** had been a writer... Yet, even in jewellery and fashion design, Jagger's rock 'n' roll heritage and haute hippy lifestyle seem to have found a good niche, that is why her first standalone shop, all dusky pink walls, dramatic black skirting and luxurious golden pillars and mirrors,

is a shrine to that decadent, yet sumptuous and elegant spirit, which includes all a girl could ask for: a fine jewellery line (cue here, gold totemic skulls and safety pins) all made in India and with prices starting at £100), as well as a collection of beautiful beaded boho-luxe dresses. DG

MAP 12 Ref. 22
Jade Jagger
43 All Saints Road
Notting Hill W11 4HE
+44 (0)20 7221 3991
www.jadejagger.co.uk.
www.iwantjezebel.co.uk
Tue–Sat 12–7pm

Notting Hill. **Fashion**

Best known as an interior designer, **Katrina Phillips** also has her own Portobello boutique where stock reflects both her impeccable taste as well as her ethical ethos. You won't find a single mass-produced product in her diverse store; instead, items are carefully sourced from around the world and chosen as much for their beauty as for their virtuous and eco credentials. Antique and new homeware range from huge pottered bowls and hand-woven baskets to petrified wood slates; while ethically made clothes and accessories include gorgeous vegetable-tanned sustainable leather handbags by Sonya Kashmiri and mud-dyed silks by Les Racines Du Ciel. These beauties don't come cheap, but there's something to be said for shopping with a clear conscience. *ZA*

MAP12 Ref. 9
Katrina Phillips
99 Portobello Road
Notting Hill W11 2QB
+44 (0)20 7229 1963
www.katrinaphillipsinteriors.com
7 Days 10–6pm
Also by appointment

-10%

On jewellery*

It may mean 'East meets West' in Japanese, but there is nothing Zen or civilised about **Kokon To Zai**. On the contrary, this fashion boutique is bordering on the bold, the surreal and the plain outrageous. You have never seen anything like this before. The 'child' of Marjan Pejoski and Sasha Bezovski, two Macedonian émigrés who came to study fashion design in London, Kokon to Zai opened its doors in 1996, originally as a space where DJs could hang out. Having gained cult status since then, Kokon to Zai now offers not just the designers' own labels 'Marjan Pejoski' (remember Bjork's famous swan dress?) and the flamboyant 'KTZ' but also a mix of clothes from fashion's most known provocateurs; Alexander McQueen, Vivienne Westwood and Jeremy Scott, to name but a few. All exhibited against a background of stuffed animals and antique paraphernalia making Kokon to Zai's eccentric microcosm an unforgettable experience. *DG*

MAP 12 Ref. 23
Kokon To Zai
86 Golborne Road
Notting Hill W10 5PS
+44 (0)20 8960 3736
www.kokontozai.co.uk
Mon–Sat 10–6pm

'I never liked zips, for some reason, or buttons.' says Peter **May**. That is why his womenswear collection features straightforward panels of fabric, which can be draped or tied around the body. 'It's easier that way,' he says. 'Not only you can be more imaginative but it's how you make a dress become truly yours.' May, who is a self-taught fashion designer, set up shop off Portobello after having worked for many prestigious fashion labels for years. His style is all about versatility and simple lines as well as a subversive attitude towards fashion: one size fits all. Here you can find an array of jersey, cotton, wool and silk dresses and tops, in a wearable palette of colours, like black, dark green, grey, navy blue and purple, all made using British fabrics as well as a range of leather accessories. Prices range from £95 to £285. *DG*

MAP 12 Ref. 20
May
61b Lancaster Road
Notting Hill W11 1QG
+44 (0)20 7229 2580
www.mayshop.co.uk
Mon–Sat 11–6pm
Sun 12–5pm

There's a delightfully playful tone in **Melt**. Themed quotes – such as 'Forget love, I'd rather fall in chocolate' – decorate the walls and the handmade treats range from serious slabs of connoisseur's chocolate to fun, gift-like options such as the brilliant Melt Mug – an illustrated mug filled with the store's legendary hot chocolate blocks-on-sticks for easy stir-and-melt. Fresh chocolates are made in house and vary with the seasons: so you might get raspberry and mint in summer or apple cider chocs come autumn. Perennial bestsellers include a lip-smacking sea salt caramel bonbon and single origin options from Venezuela, Madagascar and Papua New Guinea. There's also a great selection of 90 gram bars in intriguing flavours: Popcorn quite literally has bits of popcorn in it, while Smoke highlight's the natural tobacco notes of cocoa beans grown in volcanic soil. *ZA*

MAP 12 Ref. 11

Melt
59 Ledbury Road
Notting Hill W11 2AA
+44 (0)20 7727 5030
www.meltchocolates.com
Mon–Sat 10–6.30pm
Sun 11–4pm

Discount*

Sleek interiors, minimal decor, comfortable sofas: you'd think this was just another posh boutique for Notting Hill's boho elite. But don't let that fool you. **The Merchant** is actually a second-hand shop with a great selection of designer finds: Chanel, Gucci, Prada, Louis Vuitton but also Helmut Lang and Manolo Blahnik. Everything has passed the shop's quality control test, so do expect a lot of well kept pieces. There is even a waiting list for Hermes' Birkin bags. Capitalising on her experience as a globe-trotting personal shopper, Hamburg-born owner Vanessa Bunsen has a list of contacts who constantly feed her emporium with great stock. But with a twist: sellers have the option of donating part or all of their earnings to a preferred charity. Says Bunsen 'This way you know that when you buy anything from The Merchant, it will also benefit someone else'. A classic case of 'looking good by doing good'. *DG*

MAP 12 Ref. 10

The Merchant
36a Ledbury Road
Notting Hill W11 2AB
+44 (0)20 7229 1057
www.themerchant24.com
Mon–Sat 10.30–6pm
Sun 12–6pm

Something of a local secret, the village-like Clarendon Cross rewards intrepid shoppers with a cluster of enticing independent stores including antique boutique, **Myriad**. For some 35 years, owner Sara Fenwick has scoured markets at home and abroad and commissioned wonderful one-off pieces with the aim of filling the shop with an ever-evolving collection of antique and modern homeware. Rustic, yet stylish armchairs, dining tables and cabinets join smaller functional and ornamental pieces from eye-catching candelabras to stone birdfeeders. While you can never be sure what you might find here, returning favourites include made-to-order backgammon boards as well as a cornucopia of handcrafted mirrors. With such eclectic and beautiful stock, it's no surprise that Myriad has become a firm favourite with interior designers, not to mention west London's chicest residents. ZA

MAP 11 Ref. 4

Myriad
131 Portland Road
Clarendon Cross
Notting Hill W11 4LW
+44 (0)20 7227 1709
www.myriadantiques.com
Tues, Wed, Thur
and Sat 11–5pm

Notting Hill . **Home**

Oliver Goldsmith

Oliver Goldsmith has been described by the V&A Museum as the 'originator of fashion eyewear'. His designs have been worn by Hollywood's crème de la crème; Audrey Hepburn on Breakfast at Tiffany's, Michael Caine and Grace Kelly. Not only a shop, but more a haven for any eyewear enthusiast, Oliver Goldsmith has an extensive vintage archive of over 400 frames on display that customers can use as a reference for their own bespoke designs. Filled with nostalgic images of collaborations with the heroes of old Hollywood, it also serves as a history lesson on past fashions. Besides a bespoke service, with all frames being handmade in England and embossed with your name, if you want something extra, here you can also find the main collection of Oliver Goldsmith sunglasses, all replicas of their vintage designs as well as Claire Goldsmith's (Oliver's great grand-daughter) debut collection, called Legacy. *DG*

MAP 12 Ref. 21
Oliver Goldsmith
14 All Saints Road
Notting Hill W11 1HA
+44 (0)20 7460 0844
www.olivergoldsmith.com
Tue–Sat 10.30–6pm

Sophie Mason has come up with a winning combination of vintage threads and ethical clothes in this pretty Notting Hill boutique. The carefully curated vintage collection is handpicked by Mason and reflects her long-standing obsession with patterns, cuts and quality fabrics, while her focus on vintage tweeds and knitwear reveals her interest in traditionally manufactured English textiles. This attention to age-old craftsmanship extends to **Still**'s distinctive range of ethical clothes, produced in collaboration with various independent craftspeople in India. Stunning, hand-loomed wools, hand-embroidered detailing and hand-woven silks feature across an array of one-off items, adding extra artisan value to already beautiful contemporary designs. It makes for a clutch of gorgeous pieces that not celebrate and keep alive disappearing textile skills, but also help to support the communities, tribes and groups creating the work. ZA

MAP 12 Ref. 19
Still
61d Lancaster road
Notting Hill W11 1QG
+44 (0)20 7243 2932
www.stillethical.com
Mon–Sat 11–7pm

A homage to Britain's sartorial heritage, **Stumper & Fielding** is a treasure trove of country chic. Menswear dominates the Portobello store, with traditional tweed jackets, riding coats, polo shirts and knitwear, though a petite range of womenswear covers much the same ground. The shop's styling – think old trunks, vintage sporting props and Union Jack bunting – reflects the quintessentially English labels it celebrates and works as a fitting back drop to carefully crafted hats by Christy, quality Loake shoes and apparel by Barbour, Racing Green, Gibson, Peregrine and the like. If that's not enough English for you, try mugs in honour of Kate and Wills or tea towels embellished with bicycles and bowler hats. ZA

MAP 12 Ref. 8

Stumper & Fielding
107 Portobello Road
Notting Hill W11 2QB
+44 (0)20 7229 5577
www.stumperandfielding.com
Mon–Fri 10–6pm
Sat–Sun 9–7pm

If you ever wondered how you can give your kitchen that 'wow' factor or how you can organise the perfect dinner party, just head to **Summerill & Bishop**. Established in 1994 by longtime friends, June Summerill and Bernadette Bishop, this beautiful kitchen shop offers an amazing range of hand-crafted ceramics, bakeware, glassware, candles, monogrammed vintage linens and plates as well as some great utensils for the truly desering kitchen (think here, tarte tatin moulds and meat lifting forks).

Reflecting the allure and rustic elegance of the Provencal house or the laid-back charm of the Tuscany-style kitchen, most of the products are sourced accordingly; from France and Italy. The shop's highlight must be Its collection of 'art de la table' objects, which often include vintage finds from flea markets around Europe. As the owners say, 'it's often the little things in life that make the biggest difference.' We couldn't agree more. DG

MAP 11 Ref. 5

Summerill & Bishop
100 Portland Road
Holland Park W11 4LQ
+44 (0) 20 7221 4566
www.summerillandbishop.com
Mon–Sat 10–6pm

Notting Hill . **Home**

This two-floor gallery-cum-shop is a mecca for glass lovers. Upstairs, myriad glass bowls, vases, ornaments, lighting and sculpture cover just about every taste and budget, while downstairs a seasonally changing exhibition space presents exciting or experimental artists working in the field. The focus is on contemporary, often minimalist design and the collection is skillfully curated. It makes **Vessel** a great stop for gifts and you'll find plenty of beautiful and useful ceramic or glass objects by accessible practitioners and companies such as Lena Bergström, Lynn Read, Fornasetti and Moser. Of course, there are also more extravagant, investment items to enjoy and prices can reach into the thousands for artworks and specially commissioned pieces. ZA

MAP 12 Ref. 7

Vessel
114 Kensington Park Road
Notting Hill W11 2PW
+44 (0)20 7278 8001
www.vesselgallery.com
Tue–Sat 10–6pm

Well it's certainly no bicycle shop I can tell you that. With a nod to Colette in Paris, **The Village Bicycle** is no doubt the coolest boutique in London, it's like an exhibition of the kitsch and quirky for the exceptionally trendy. Alongside Japanese collectable toys and Nike Air Max trainers they stock underground labels like Felder Felder, Mark Fast, Ashish and Marjan Pejoski alongside Mexican Day of the Dead memorabilia and Lady Gaga sunglasses proving that the buyers here have a sixth sense for extreme style. Lit up like a warped Christmas tree with Perspex cases full of rubber snakes and a wall of fluorescent crosses and display cabinets, this store will delight all out there with a love of tattoos, leather jackets and diamante studded iPhone covers. *PB*

MAP 12 Ref. 15
The Village Bicycle
79–81 Ledbury Road
Notting Hill W11 2AG
+44 (0)20 7792 8601
www.imavillagebicycle.com
Mon–Sat 11–7pm

Notting Hill . *Fashion*

Wolf & Badger

Brothers Henry and George Graham are behind this concept store founded in early 2010, which has quickly become a Notting Hill classic; in less than a year it has even won Vogue's prestigious 'Best Boutique' accolade. Its philosophy? Rather than exhibiting and selling established artists and designers, **Wolf & Badger** have created a platform for fostering and promoting exciting, new independent talent. Freeing them from the financial worries of opening their own store, even helping them with distribution, manufacturing and press. Expect to find a truly unique and idiosyncratic selection of womenswear, menswear, accessories, jewellery and even some stunning interiors pieces. *DG*

MAP 12 Ref. 12

Wolf & Badger
46 Ledbury Road
Notting Hill W11 2AB
+44 (0)20 7229 5698
www.wolfandbadger.com
Mon–Sat 10–6pm
Sun 11–5pm

You want a beautifully carved baroque bed covered in silver leaf? Or a Louis XIV cabinet with a sprayed 'Imperfect' on it? Maybe a carver chair in Union Jack- inspired upholstery? Whatever your demand, turn to Jimmie Karlsson and Martin Nihlmar, of **Jimmie Martin**, for some luxury DIY. Their speciality is taking French style furniture and giving them the 'upcycle' spin, slightly quirky, slightly kitsch but thoroughly unique, which means they create one-off pieces which they customise with fun and funky

new upholstery, finishes, hand-painted images and spray-painted graffiti. You can choose from an array of existing designs or request your own frame finish, upholstery and artwork. DG

MAP 11 Ref. 2

Jimmie Martin
77 Kensington Church Street
Kensington W8 4BG
+44 (0)20 7938 1852
www.jimmiemartin.co.uk
Mon–Fri 11–6pm
Sat 12–4pm

Kensington . **Home**

175

'The main aesthetic at **Pomegranate** is clean simple lines and an emphasis on hand-crafted organic forms,' says Katie Bulatovic, owner of this gem of a jewellery shop, which she opened back in 2008. Beautiful silver bracelets, necklaces and rings with natural gemstones, like aquamarines and smokey quartz are a highlight. So is the price. Starting at just £15, people here can experiment with pieces that are different or pieces that work with current trends, without having to make a big investment – 'but still purchasing something in precious metal and set with gemstones; something that has an intrinsic value and a story behind it,' as Bulatovic puts it. Everything is sourced in India, Thailand and Turkey from local craftsmen and artisans, so expect a unique range of wonderful stones, techniques and styles. *DG*

MAP 11 Ref. 1
Pomegranate
8 Kensington Square
Kensington W8 5EP
+44 (0)20 7937 9735
www.pomegranate-london.co.uk
Mon–Sat 10–6pm
Sun 12–5pm

Eulabee is Verandah's younger sister. Opened in 2008, just around the corner from its predecessor, this magnificent emporium is based on the same principles: beautiful, retro and slightly quirky but above all affordable. Simone Russell and Penny Meachin have done a wonderful job at creating not just a shop but rather a funky and laid back lifestyle. The shop is superbly staged with all the objects on sale, which adds to Eulabee's thoroughly charming and slightly eccentric spirit. The focus here is on homeware (cushions, cake stands and other decorative objects as well as design books and even table games), while the whole experience feels like a fun day out: from the fake grass patch on the outside to the adjacent cafe where you can have a delicious lunch or enjoy a quick cup of coffee. Bonus: the shop is very child-friendly. *DG*

MAP 13 Ref. 29

Eulabee
116 College Road
Kensal Rise NW10 5HD
+44 (0)20 8968 5536
Mon–Sat 10–6pm
Sun 10–4pm

Kensal Rise . *Home*

Corina Papadopoulou was an MTV producer before she opened one of London's most lovable children's boutiques. And she couldn't have found a better place to do it: after all, NW10 is a notorious Nappy Valley. Yet there is something different in her approach. "When I conceived the idea for **Kidsen**, I was heavily pregnant with my first child. Getting ready for my daughter's arrival, I was tired of shops which treat kids like grown-ups or ones that try to sell you everything" says this half-Greek,

half-Swedish mother of two. That is why Kidsen, which opened in 2008, is not just a shop but more of 'a friendly community'. 'Here you can meet other mums and get advice on breastfeeding or the best nappies.' On top of that, Kidsen also stocks an eclectic range of Scandinavian baby- and childrenswear ('functional and practical without being ugly') as well as some wonderful toys. *DG*

MAP 13 Ref. 27
Kidsen
111 Chamberlayne Road
Kensal Rise NW10 3NS
+44 (0)20 8969 7565
www.kidsen.co.uk
Mon–Fri 10–5.30pm
Sat 10–5pm

Fashion designer Nelli Turner has already had a varied and interesting life; from an idyllic childhood in Bavaria to her studies at the Ecole Superieure d'Arts Appliques in Geneva and finally to her arrival in London, where she has worked for designer duo Clements Ribeiro. As such, her Kensal Rise boutique, **Lali**, is a testament to this unique lifestyle. Besides stocking her own Bi La Li womenswear brand, which she founded in 2001 (modern design and clean silhouettes are a signature style) Lali plays host to an amazing selection of young, savvy and original clothes, like Ghulam Sakina dresses, Eley Kishimoto and Osman Yousefzada separates, quirky jewellery by Tatty Devine and Mawi as well as Ally Cappelino accessories. Besides its unique retail offerings, here you can also find an array of objects from upcoming designers, design graduates and artists. In other words, a 'must see'. *DG*

MAP 13 Ref. 25

Lali
15 Station Terrace
Kensal Rise NW10
+44 (0)20 8968 9130
www.bilali.com
Tue–Thu 11–7pm
Fri–Sat 10–7pm
Sun 11–5pm

Kensal Rise · **Fashion**

With just a handful of rails and a pocket-sized space, **Love KR** owner Paula Fitzpatrick has created a one-stop shop for all your fashion needs. Her bijou, Kensal Rise boutique offers a brilliantly edited selection of appealing apparel sourced from independent and emerging designers and labels. Highlights include jeans by LA brand Paige, feminine day wear by French label Des Petits Hauts and edgy threads by Eleven Paris. Jewellery (there are some great pieces by Bex Rox) as well as accessories and shoes by labels such as H by Hudson and Isle Jacobson complete the bounty you'll find here. As an added perk, Paula herself is often on hand with good advice and a keen eye for a distinctive outfit. *ZA*

MAP 13 Ref. 28

LoveKR
98 Chamberlayne Road
Kensal Rise NW10 3JN
+44 (0)20 8962 5635
www.lovekr.co.uk
Tues–Sat 10.30–7pm
Sun 11–5pm

Adam Hills and Maria Speake met as architecture students, got married and founded **Retrouvius**, an interior design practice and showroom with an interesting design manifesto: there is no such thing as waste. Case in point, their studio, which is made from reused materials and salvage. Hills, Speake and their team scour the UK for old buildings, be it soon-to-be demolished schools, galleries and even museums and take back anything that can be put into a new context; like the fossilised marble floor found at a demolished Heathrow terminal (which was subsequently made into a bathtub and a coffee table). Other reclaimed objects include cupboards, lighting, mirrors, as well as garden accessories. The great thing is that stock is ever changing, so chances are that you will find something unique and quirky, like the Central Line's old tube signs. Incredible to think that these were unwanted. *DG*

MAP 13 Ref. 24

Retrouvius
2A Ravensworth Road
Kensal Green NW10 5NR
+44 (0)20 8960 6060
www.retrouvious.com
Mon–Sat 10–6pm

Kensal Green . *Home*

Friends Simone Russell and Penny Meachin have always wanted to create a shop with 'unusual but beautiful things'. So, having had a background in textiles and fashion design respectively, they opened **Verandah** back in 2000, a gorgeous little place full of beautiful gifts and treats as well as funky womenswear. Originally in Notting Hill, Verandah has since then moved to NW10 but has still retained its retro charm, quirky attitude and affordability factor. Here you will love the great selection of 'pocket money' ideas, such as lip salves, mirrored compacts, all starting at 50p, but also the amazing second-hand designer bargains.
The shop itself is an explosion of colour and patterns: the diamond-shaped print on the floor as well as the colourful treats Russell and Meachin have chosen for Verandah are simply a feast for the eyes. It helps that the latter are affordable, too. *DG*

MAP 13 Ref. 26
Verandah
117 Chamberlayne Road
Kensal Rise NW10 3NS
+44 (0)20 8968 5498
Mon–Sat 10–6pm
Sun 12–5pm

Aelia Laelia

Aelia Laelia is one of those retail institutions that have remained true to the original Chelsea spirit: a real independent boutique with unique designers who make fashion that extends beyond the current trends. This little treasure cave specialises in womenswear that is 'fun, happy, colourful and practical', as owner, Cathy Rayner, says. With a background in textile design and fashion sales, Rayner's ethos is all about offering quality brands that 'you can't find anywhere else', something which translates into timeless fashion from

an eclectic and not widely available range of English, French and Danish names. Its speciality? Its extensive selection of great tops and dresses, with prices starting at just £49. Aelia Laelia is also known for its amazing holidaywear all year around; Star Mela kaftans, leather boho sandals, cute studded belts. Judging by its cool and laidback vibe, now we know why. *DG*

MAP 14 Ref. 33

Aelia Laelia
4 Cale Street
Chelsea SW3 3QU
+44 (0)20 7584 4400
Mon–Sat 10–6pm

Chelsea . *Fashion*

15%

Discount*

182

A girl's heaven on earth! **Austique** is filled with utterly feminine clothes, fabulous jewellery, cheeky accessories and every day necessities: from Libelula dresses, Wilbur and Gussie's chic pochettes and Alex Monroe's bumblebee necklaces, to Seda France's scented candles, cashmere gloves, Essie nail varnishes and New York's infamous Dylan's Candy Bar goodies. The best thing? Its relaxed yet thoroughly glam atmosphere. It feels like you are in your private boudoir, sharing secrets and tips with your best friend just before a great night out. Owners are sisters Lindy Lopes and Katie Canvin, who opened Austique back in 2004 and whose aim was to introduce niche Australian brands into the habits of style conscious Chelsea girls. Since then, Austique has grown into a prime destination for original and thoroughly feminine fashion brands. *DG*

MAP 14 Ref. 36

Austique
330 King's Road
Chelsea SW3 5UR
+44 (0)20 7376 4555
www.austique.co.uk
Mon–Sat 10:30–7pm
Sun 12–5pm

Hot on the latest craze for all things traditional, **The Chelsea Teapot** is all about serving the best English afternoon tea with a slice of moist Victoria sponge cake, in a place that you feel as if time has stopped. Oozing old school charm, with yummy cupcake coloured walls, a stall full of glass stands featuring the best and most scrumptious cakes, scones and jelly beans and a group of friendly ladies behind the counter, you won't be able to resist. Did we mention that home-made gluten and wheat free cupcakes and sandwiches are on offer too? Here you can also find the cutest little accessories for serving the perfect 'tea' at home: from cupcake-inspired mugs to cute candles and funky cake and chocolate decorations. 'A little heaven' indeed. DG

MAP 14 Ref. 37

The Chelsea Teapot
402 Kings Road
Chelsea SW10 0LJ
+44 (0)20 7751 5975
www.thechelseateapot.com
Tue–Fri 8.30–6.30pm
Sat 9.30–6.30pm
Sun 12–6.30pm

Chelsea . *Cafe*

Felt

If you are looking for something special – that eternity ring with those ethically sourced uncut gemstones by Pippa Small, or that one of a kind necklace with oversized links by Taher Chemirik, even those vintage 18-carat gold earrings - but you don't have the time to visit hidden away shops and faraway studios or the strength to do the flea market scene, just head over to **Felt**, an Alladin's cave but for jewellery. Its owner Eliza Poklewski Koziell, a specialist who used to work for auction/vintage obsessed entrepreneurs, has selected designers who may be lesser known but they nevertheless feature a unique design sensibility. What is great about Felt is also the fact that it is unassuming and casual; jewellery is treated not as something to be marvelled at from afar or behind glass cases but rather something that you should try on and make work for you. Prices range from £20 to £10,000, while you can also sell your old jewellery through the shop and get a credit for the amount they were sold for. *DG*

MAP 14 Ref. 34

Felt
13 Cale Street
Chelsea SW3 3QS
+44 (0)20 7349 8829
www.felt-london.com
Mon–Sat 10–6pm

'Effortlessly cool, creative clothes, for independent, hard-working, fun, busy women.' This is the mantra of Fi Lovett, owner of **Fifi Wilson**. Sounds too good to be true? Well, not really. Unless you haven't made it to her Chelsea outpost yet. Filled with designer clothes, accessories and jewellery, all items have a retro, nostalgic charm and include feminine and cute labels such as Manoush, Antoni Alison, Sonia Rykiel, Vivetta and Elizabeth Lau, among others. Fifi Wilson's strength lies in its laid back attitude. You are free to check out merchandise without being hassled by annoying members of staff, in an environment that is above all friendly and welcoming. All in all, this is a great shopping destination for original, trendy and utterly charming clothes. *DG*

MAP 14 Ref. 35
Fifi Wilson
1 Godfrey Street
Chelsea SW3 3TA
+44 (0)20 7352 3232
www.fifiwilson.com
Mon–Sat 10–6pm

As soon as you come near the shop, you feel as if you are about to enter a Buddhist temple: the air is filled with the exotic aroma of incense sticks. For **Opium** is a temple to the marvels of India. For over ten years, Terry Kitching has been trawling the Indian sub-continent, assembling unique treasures, which form the core of this amazing and thoroughly unique shop. Expect to find stone and wood temple pillars, palace doors from Rajasthan, colonial beds from Calcutta, stunning mirrors made from 18th century carved doorway frames, marble elephants from Udaipur as well as Hindu deities carved in marble from Varanasi. Opium also stocks more affordable offerings, such as door knobs made of colonial porcelain, old spice boxes as well as silk bed throws made by craftspeople in the villages of Rajasthan, Gujarat and Uttar Pradesh. *DG*

MAP 14 Ref. 38

Opium
414 Kings Road
Chelsea SW10 0LJ
+44 (0)20 7795 0700
www.opiumshop.co.uk
Mon–Sat 10–6.30pm
Sun 12–5pm

When you enter this small establishment, you feel as if you have stepped into a Roald Dahl or Beatrix Potter fairytale. Beautifully made pieces of furniture and huge Victorian doll houses dominate the space, evoking a nostalgic kind of charm. **Dragons of Walton Street** is a family business from Sussex, starting out 30 years ago, when Rosie Fisher started commissioning hand-painted furniture for her children. Today it offers not just beautifully hand-painted bespoke furniture, but whole design ideas for imaginative children's bedrooms and playrooms; and it doesn't stop there. Details such as personalised hairbrushes with a favourite cartoon hero, union jack themed-beds and even miniature Louis XIV sofas featuring fairies are also on offer. It may not come cheap, yet every piece will be a memory that any child will cherish for life. *DG*

MAP 14 Ref. 31
Dragons of Walton Street
23 Walton Street
Knightsbridge SW3 2HX
+44 (0)20 7589 3795
www.dragonsofwaltonstreet.com
Mon–Fri 9.30–5.30pm
Sat 10–5pm

Few and Far

You may get the impression that you have just come to a glossy modern art gallery of the Saatchi calibre instead: all wide open spaces and quirky installations. But these are not Charles Saatchi's new 'Sensations' rather than Priscilla Carluccio's unique selection of designers and artisans. The ex-wife of restaurateur Antonio and sister of design impresario Terence Conran, Priscilla has accumulated some serious credentials over the years. After all, she was the driving force behind two lifestyle successes, The Conran Shop and Habitat. Recently, she has been putting all her energy into a new project; **Few and Far**, that is, a furniture and lifestyle store with a cosmopolitan view on design. Expect here the usual 'suspects', like furniture by Paola Navone or Cappellini but with a quirky detail thrown into the mix: a knit dress from the Faroe Islands, a stool brought over from India or a metal cantelabra from Senegal. *DG*

MAP 14 Ref. 30
Few and Far
242 Brompton Road
Chelsea SW3 2BB
+44 (0)20 7225 7070
www.fewandfar.net
Mon–Sat 10 – 6pm
Sun 12–5pm

Sarah Mahaffy describes herself as one of retail's 'late bloomers'. After all, before she opened **Maharani**, back in 2006, she had carved a 27-year career in book publishing. As the name suggests (maharani is the wife of a maharajah, an Indian prince), her SW3 emporium specialises in a wide yet exclusive selection of clothes and accessories, like silk jackets, cashmere shawls, jewellery, home accessories (bedspreads and quilts) as well as antique textiles from the Indian sub-continent, especially from exotic places like Jaipur and Hyderabad. 'We aim to show our customers just some of the riches that are to be found there.' Mahaffy says. If you want to delve into Indian craftsmanship more, Maharani hold special events during the year, some of which include talks on textiles. *DG*

MAP 14 Ref. 32
Maharani
173 Fulham Road
South Kensington SW3 6JW
+44 (0)20 7581 0769
www.maharanitrading.com
Mon–Sat 10–6pm
Wed till 7pm
Sun 12–5pm

-5%

Discount on purchases over £100*

Samuel Chan is a Hong-Kong born, UK furniture design graduate that has carved a name in the design world for his organic style and his superb hand-finished furniture. His bright, zen-like showroom and studio, called **Channels** is testament to the spirit of this design genius, who created his first product, 'Rocking Chair' as a present to his mother, when he was just 15. Chan's impressive CV includes designing furniture for luxury hotels like the Lanesborough, and iconic furniture shops, like Heals the iconic furniture store as well as pieces for gallery shows. Chan's trademark style: natural materials such as wood which he explores in original, interesting and 'progressive' ways, showcasing an approach to design, which is all about 'less is more'. Among the shop's highlights are the 'motley drums', a series of furniture with multi-functional character (seats that can be used as tables and vice versa), which actually look like drums, all made from reclaimed and sustainable materials. *DG*

MAP 15 Ref. 39

Channels
1-3 New King's Road
Fulham SW6 4SB
+44 (0)20 7371 0301
www.channelsdesign.com
Mon–Sat 10–5.30pm

Deuxieme abides perfectly by the adage 'One person's unwanted item is another's treasure'. This small shopping haunt specialises in second-hand fashion whether you are a buyer or a seller. Some of the items on sale include highly desirable names like Jimmy Choo, Frost French, Prada, Gucci but also top high street labels like LK Bennett as well as vintage pieces at really affordable prices; at a recent trip, for example we found a pink Luella cardigan for £39 and a Louis Vuitton bag for £75. Stock is renewed daily and is extensive: from shoes to beautiful art deco costume jewellery and accessories. You could literally spend hours in here; not only is there a cute garden cafe where you can take a fair-trade coffee break (clutching that Prada dress of course, you don't want someone else to get it) but also there is free wifi so you can stay updated on what's going on outside. *DG*

MAP 15 Ref. 41

Deuxieme
299 New King's Road
Fulham SW6 4RE
+44 (0)20 7736 3696
www.deuxieme.co.uk
Mon–Sat 10–6pm
Sun 11–5pm

Blame it all on a trip to India. That's all it took Ruth Kehoe and her friend Karin Andreasson to recreate a second **Indian Summer** in 2004, a beautiful 'lifestyle' boutique whose actual vibe transports you to the casual and buzzy Indian bazaars. For a start, the pink exterior blows you away, as it prepares you for the vibrant and thoroughly feminine paradise that you will encounter inside. This includes not just clothes, but a quirky mix of homewares, jewellery, children's toys and beauty products, all sourced from upcoming and unique labels. Some of the perennial bestsellers include the ever popular mid-length cotton kaftans (£25), silk pashminas imported from India (59.95) imported from India, candles, cups, furniture, coin necklaces (£31), cute knitted berry hats (£17.95) and rattles (£10.50) for your little ones. Honestly, you won't be able to get out of there holding just one item. *DG*

MAP 15 Ref. 43

Indian Summer
624c Fulham Road
Fulham SW6 5RS
+44 (0)20 7731 8234
www.indiansummershop.com
Mon–Sat 10–6.30pm
Sun 12–5pm

Fed up with the routine of their daily jobs, longtime friends, Jo Thyne and Katie Broadbent decided to spice up their lives by doing their own thing. Having lived in Parsons Green for years, it was at a dinner when they came up with the idea for **Katie & Jo** a boutique with clothes and accessories that caters to the stylish needs of 30 to 45 year-old women (mothers and professionals alike). The concept is based on bringing feminine, contemporary brands from the US, Australia, France and Sweden, especially ones that are not widely available in London. Much of the selection also showcases their complimentary relationship: Broadbent is a fan of the 'Parisian chic', while Thyne likes clothes with an edgy touch. Among the 'treasures' you can find here, are art-nouveau inspired wedges from Cleo B, Sretsis easy going separates, Superfine jeans, bohemian Shakuhachi dresses and statement jewellery by Bex Rox. *DG*

MAP 15 Ref. 40
Katie & Jo
253 New King's Road
Fulham SW6 4RB
+44 (0)20 7736 5304
www.katieandjo.com
Mon–Wed 10–7pm
Thu 10–8pm Fri 10–6pm
Sat–Sun 10–5pm

Let's say you have signed up for the London marathon and you need a pair of running shoes but the sort of pair that doesn't give you blisters. Or the sort of pair, which minimises pain and increases your performance. 'Does it really exist,' you may ask. Well, it actually does. Just head to **Profeet**, London's premium makers of custom-made running shoes. Their personal advice service uses cutting edge technology which analyses your biomechanics, your activity, your movement as well as any injuries

history, and will deliver the right solution: a pair of shoes specially designed for your needs. Profeet also provides the same service for many other adrenaline inducing sports, such as skiing, cycling and even climbing. The end result as attested by its loyal fans: more power transfer and comfort. No pain, no gain? That's now a myth. DG

MAP 15 Ref. 42

Profeet

867-869 Fulham Road

Fulham SW6 5HP

+44 (0)20 3411 9782

www.profeet.co.uk

Mon–Fri 10–6pm

Tue–Thu 10–8pm

Sat 9–6pm Sun 10–4pm

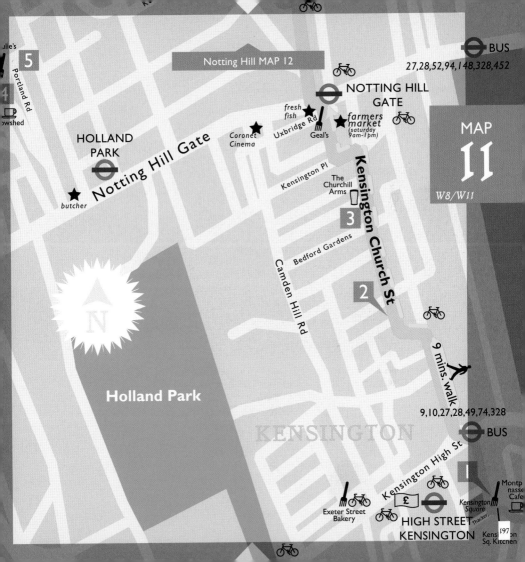

BUS
27,28,52,94,148,328,452

NOTTING HILL GATE

MAP
11

W8/W11

HOLLAND
PARK

fresh fish

Uxbridge Rd

farmers market
(saturday 9am–1pm)

Coronet
Cinema

Geal's

Notting Hill Gate

Notting Hill Gate

butcher

Kensington Pl

The Churchill Arms

Kensington Church St

3

Bedford Gardens

Camden Hill Rd

2

9 mins. walk

9,10,27,28,49,74,328

KENSINGTON

BUS

Holland Park

N

Kensington High St

Exeter Street Bakery

£

Kensington Square

Thacker

Montpnasse Cafe

1

HIGH STREET
KENSINGTON

Kensi...on
Sq. Kitchen

197

Julie's

5

Portland Rd

4

owshed

MAP
12
W11

Golbo

Great cafes and street food

23

Westway

market (Saturdays)

WESTBOURNE
PARK

Oxford Gardens

Tavistock Rd

The Pelican

All Saints Road

Great Western Rd

Lucky Seven

The Cow

The Westbourne

Gusto Cafe

22

Lancaster Rd

Westbourne Pk Rd

Crazy Homies

Rosa's

Westbourne Pk Rd

Chepstow Rd

21

19 **20**

Essenza

Books for Cooks

E & O

17

16

Talbot Rd

The Ledbury

LADBROKE
GROVE

Travel bookshop

Electric Cinema

Colville Terrace

Ledbury Rd

Walmer Castle

Cock & Bottle

Otto Pizza

Blenhem Crescent

Cafe Respiro

15

14

Westbourne Grove

St Petersburgh Pl

grocer

18

Lonsdale Rd

Tom's Deli

Ottolenghi

Ladbroke Grove

Kensington Pk Rd

Lutyens Rubinstein

Portobello Rd

11

12

13

8

10

Beach blanket Babylon

Pembridge Villas

NOTTING HILL

7 **9**

Dawson Pl

Moscow Road

BAYSW

MAP

13

NW10

BUS
187,52,6,302

The Chamberlayne

KENSAL RISE

Chamberlayne Rd

KENSAL RISE

laceland

29

The Island

KENSAL GREEN

Harvist Road

27

28

25 Minkie's Deli

26

★ *Brooks butchers*

16 mins. walk

Kilburn Lane

Lessy's

Mortimer Road

KENSAL GREEN

WEST KILBURN

24

Harrow Road

Kensal Green Cemetery

Paradise

The Regent

Regent st.

Grand Union Canal

Ladbroke Road

BUS
18,N18

Harrow Road

KENSAL TOWN

N

MAP
14

SW5/SW3

Harrods

KNIGHTSBRIDGE

Science Museum

Brompton Quarter Cafe

Pont St

Merchant's Yard

Beauchamp Pl

al History Museum

Cromwell Road

30

Brompton Rd

Walton St

31

The Enterprise

Cadogan Square

GLOUCESTER ROAD

Farmers Market
(Saturday 9am-2pm)

La Brasserie

Jack's

SLOANE SQUARE

Harrington Gardens

Gloucester Road

SOUTH KENSINGTON

Old Brompton Rd

Admiral Codrington

Draycott Ave

Draycott Pl

SM Sc

32

Sloane Ave

Whiteheads Grove

BUS
430,C1

Drayston Gardens

Royal Marsden Hospital

Elystan St

grocer

Saatchi Gallery

CHELSEA

33

Album

Cale St

BUS
11,19,22,211

Sydney St

34

35

Markham

Old Church St

The Trafalgar

Kings Rd

Belocq

Fulham Rd

23 mins. walk

The Phene

Oakley St

Park walk

36

8 over 8

Buonasera

Chelsea Embankment

Love Cake

Edith Grove

Beaufort St

37

38

Kings Rd

Battersea

Albert Bridge

Batterse

N

Battersea Park

200

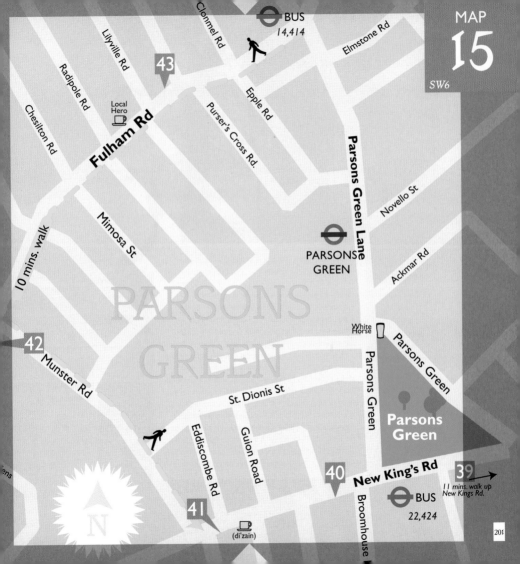

MAP
15

SW6

Clonmel Rd

Lilyville Rd

BUS
14,414

Elmstone Rd

43

Radipole Rd

Local
Hero

Fulham Rd

Purser's Cross Rd.

Epple Rd

Chesilton Rd

Parsons Green Lane

Novello St

Mimosa St

PARSONS
GREEN

Ackmar Rd

10 mins. walk

PARSONS

GREEN

42

White
Horse

Parsons Green

Munster Rd

St. Dionis St

Parsons Green

**Parsons
Green**

Eddiscombe Rd

Guion Road

40

New King's Rd

39

11 mins. walk up
New Kings Rd.

41

(di'zain)

BUS
22,424

Broomhouse

N

ens

Often seen as a place to escape the hubbub without actually leaving the city, **North London** houses its fair share of young, eco-conscious families settling down in leafy, village-like surrounds. Farmers' markets naturally abound, from Stoke Newington's all-organic market on Saturdays, to Islington's Sunday morning affair absorbed within the more general Chapel Market. The emphasis on quality food doesn't stop there: the area is heaving with family-friendly gastro pubs (The Old Dairy on the outskirts of Crouch End for classic British grub with a modern twist), quality restaurants (you can't beat Exmouth Market stalwart Moro for Moorish cuisine and independent cafes – there's a run of great stops up Regents Park Road in Primrose Hill, though Japanese patisserie Lanka is particularly worth a visit. Or for a city view try Dalston roof park.

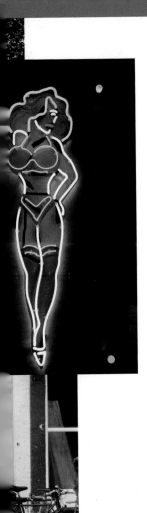

N1 *Islington*

N1 *Angel*

EC1 *Exmouth Market*

NW1 *Primrose Hill*

N10 *Muswell Hill*

N10 *Crouch End*

N16 *Stoke Newington*

N16 *Newington Green*

NORTH

This song to contemporary design is housed in the erstwhile Barnsbury Hall, a lofty space of many levels. Beautifully converted from an 1850s music and meeting hall, it's notable for being the venue that saw a young Michael Collins sworn into the Irish Republican Brotherhood. Today, a spirit of patriotism infuses the choice of home-grown products at **Aria**. Alongside the ubiquitous Euro contenders Starck, Kartell, Alessi et al, British design and manufacture is strongly represented by Anthony Dickens, Black + Blum,

Barber Osgerby, Owen Barry, John Smedley, Vivienne Westwood, Adam Aaronson, Lush Designs, Highland Tweeds, Tweedmill and others. Recipe books are from the revered taste buds at Moro, The Eagle and Leon. There's lighting, homewares, gifts and furniture. Jewellery has a shelf of its own, literally a mezzanine above the main floor. Staff are likely to be moonlighting designers and are wonderfully knowledgeable about the products. *GT*

MAP 17 Ref. 19
Aria
Barnsbury Hall
Barnsbury Street
Islington N1 1PN
+44 (0)20 7704 6222
www.ariashop.co.uk
Mon–Fri 10–6.30pm
Sun 10–6.30pm
Sun 12–6pm

Green and Fay's showroom showcases its kitchens and own-line furniture among lovely household frippery, artfully curated as if in a gallery. Seriously grown up pieces – a Hille Plan sideboard (£2040) and Fritz Hansen armchair (reupholstered in Paul Smith fabric £825) rub along happily with Pantone mugs, irreverent posters and a porcelain flower grenade (£12) on a hand-drawn mantlepiece. The punchline is you can be grown up without losing your elan vital. And how. The staff in their concept store will help you floor-plan, design and execute your dream kitchen. Or help you buy a pair of knitted eyeballs to adorn a cushion. Ardent supporters of young British designers, their till might trill £1.25 for a screenprinted birthday card, and then £1,295 for a master-crafted industrial table with steel grid hotplates. We didn't know whether to shop or clap. *TT*

MAP 17 Ref. 14
Green and Fay
137-139 Essex Road
Islington N1 2NR
+44 (0)20 7704 0455
www.greenandfay.co.uk
Mon by appointment
Tues–Sat 10–6pm

Handmade and Found

Nothing from **Handmade and Found** is ever, just so. There will always be something – a gather here, a bias cut there, a subtle subversion – that sets it apart. And then there is the quality. Oh, the quality. Heavily influenced by a Japanese ethic of fabrics being as central as design, pieces are enduring. On the day I visit I am wearing a 12 year old pair of their trousers, barely aged despite my best efforts. Owner Anthony has eschewed the workroom out back (and their old label with it) and today there is a well-

spaced, impeccably sourced vintage rail instead. (His pride and joy.) Rare Westwood and Comme des Garçons – unworn or as new – are the cherries on top of regular collections including many Japanese labels which range in price from £39 to £200. Always quality, never humdrum and often with tailoring twists which surprise – long arms, no arms, kimono sleeves and stirrup tights (cutaway heels and toes) - pieces are exclusive and produced in lovingly small numbers or as one offs. Unique, boutique, magnifique. *TT*

MAP 17 Ref. 12

Handmade and Found
109 Essex Road
Islington N1 2SL
+44 (0)20 7359 3898
www.handmadeandfound.com
Mon–Sat 10.30–6pm

Discount*

Look for the gold lettering of 193 Berwick above the door and you've found it. **Labour of Love**, that is, who stuck with the original Victorian signage because it was so damn lovely. And that sets the tone for everything else, from the wonky doorway and mosaic entrance to the quirky clothes and off-beat accessories, stocked solely on the basis of loveliness rather than a slavish need to conform to some didactic trend forecast. The buying bias is on a scale of chic to Dada, shown in their early championing of knitwear labels such as Kind and Yang Du and a fondness for colour and strong prints as manifest in the likes of Manish Arora, Ashish and Miriam Ocariz. Such gorgeous and well-made pieces have a longevity of style that will last seasons and team well with Labour of Love's own label shoes and accessories, exclusive to their shop and website. *GT*

MAP 17 Ref. 18

Labour of Love
193 Upper Street
Islington N1 2RQ
+44 (0)20 7354 9333
www.labour-of-love.co.uk
Mon–Fri 11–6.30pm
Sat 10.30–6.30pm
Sun 12–5.30pm

Discount*

For the busy and impatient aspiring crafter, **The Make Lounge** has a solution. Create a silver filigree ring, a fascinator or a bag in just one class! Too good to be true? Better believe it. Master your sewing machine by way of making an apron. Find your way around the overlocker to perfect a stretch t-shirt. Screen-print a tea-towel, bind a book, alter your jeans: all in an evening. No need to sign up for the usual term of classes that you know you'll never attend. Better still, rather than a cold classroom or church hall, sessions are held in the purpose-designed comfort of The Make Lounge with sustaining snacks and drinks to fuel the creative fire. It's a super sociable space and the adjacent shop has all the bits you need to continue making at home, along with inspiring books to keep that new-found talent burning. *GT*

MAP 17 Ref. 20

The Make Lounge
49-51 Barnsbury Street
Islington N1 1TP
+44 (0)20 7609 0275
www.themakelounge.com

The folk at **Mosquito Bikes** are wide-eyed at the ever-increasing mass of cyclists powering past their door on Essex Road. When they opened over 25 years ago everyone was known to them at least by sight and the community was clubby. Having grown up with the trend, their wealth of cycle know-how is vast and cyclists new, weary, muddy or fast will all find their service and range of bikes hard to beat. Mosquito also has two qualified Serotta Bike Fit Technicians available for SizeCycle assessments. Whether you're spending thousands on a bike or just hours in the saddle this 2 hour analysis ensures injury-free cycling by adjusting the geometry of a bike to match your individual size and style of movement. As standard, this comes free with the purchase of a more expensive bike but a session can also be booked to fit and correct an existing bike that's causing problems. *GT*

MAP 17 Ref. 13

Mosquito Bikes
123 Essex Road
Islington N1 2SN
+44 (0)20 7226 8765
www.mosquito-bikes.co.uk
Mon–Fri 8.30–7pm
Sat 10–6pm

Islington · **Bicycles**

At this flagship restaurant the line of conviviality extends from the seated diners at the long communal tables through the elegant tasters perched at the bar to the waves of customers rolling up to take away from the most sumptuously laden counter in North London. The proof is in the variety of the converted: a couple in their 80s enjoying a pre-theatre supper, girls from the office sharing mezze plates, a bloke in jeans, men in dark suits, family groups. At the tables outside, laughing mothers with smiling babies eat cake and from the other side of the road a woman dices with a speeding police car, her eyes only for **Ottolenghi** and its luscious tarts. Everyone loves this place with its noisy Mediterranean flavours. The secret's already out. All that's to add is the lesser known fact that on Upper Street they take bookings for dinner. So relax. *GT*

MAP 17 Ref. 16

Ottolenghi
287 Upper Street
Islington N1 2TZ
+44 (0)20 7288 1454
www.ottolenghi.co.uk
Mon–Sat 8–11pm
Sun 9–7pm

At **The Sampler**, first and foremost, one samples. This way you get the good stuff, that is, the stuff that you like. Rather than the stuff with the pretty label, or the bottle on promotion. The point being that taste is a personal thing. It's fine to take advice, even from the man in the shop, but ultimately the best wine is chosen by you. So top up a card and get slurping. Everyone else is. Afternoons here aren't dissimilar to a party and it's good to work the room. With over 1500 hand-picked wines on offer and a fortnightly rotation of 80 in the machines ready to sample at any one time it'll be a while before boredom hits. Should direction be called for, staff are knowledgeable and can confidently chart a course through the rare vintages, unusual places of origin and little-known vineyards. *GT*

MAP 17 Ref. 17

The Sampler
266 Upper Street
Islington N1 2UQ
+44 (0)20 7226 9500
www.thesampler.co.uk
Mon–Sat 11.30–9pm
Sun 11.30–7pm

Islington . **Wine & Beer**

Somewhere between Upper Street and Oslo is **Wild Swans**. A small corridor of calm where the lines are crisp, the air is rarefied and the complexions are clear. Native Denmark is owner Caroline van Luthje's inspiration and 95 per cent of her labels are Scandinavian as well as most of her staff. Signature Scandinavian style abounds - Materials are high end and enduring, palettes are muted (lots of nude, calico, whites and navy) and fashion never strays into frivolity but stays underpinned by stylish utility (a reversible sheepskin gillet with black leather pockets £190.) Rails are full of capsule pieces – jackets, skirts, blouses, boots – and for prettier evening wear think understated, diaphanous beauty – a sheer navy blouse with stars (£159). Pundits call it one of the best selection of Scandinavian fashion in London. Certainly it feels elevated from the urban, London high street on which it sits. A gust of crisp, alpine air in N1. *TT*

MAP 17 Ref. 15

Wild Swans
54 Cross Street
Islington N1 2BA
+44 (0)20 7354 8681
www.wild-swans.com
Mon–Sat 10–6pm
Sun 12–5pm

Champagne served on weekends*

They don't make retro like they used to. At **Fat Faced Cat** the perfumed air is redolent of a private members club or chi-chi boutique. And the scene set is worthy of a Merchant Ivory film with leather luggage, 1930s ephemera and gentlemen's formal accessories dressing the windows. 'Sophisticated vintage' is their stock, claim the owners and they carry the couture names to back it up. Despite this, they're not slaves to labels. There's nothing to stop an M&S handbag turning up on the rails if the look and quality is right.

The range is Victorian to 1980s and might include a mid '60s wiggle-dress from LA, a hand-stitched cashmere jacket by Lanvin or a 1950s blonde mink cape, all hand-picked by the owners at antique and vintage fairs in the UK and LA. Should explain why the fashion industry have already sniffed it out. *GT*

MAP 17 Ref. 11
Fat Faced Cat
22-24 Camden Passage
Islington N1 8ED
+44 (0)20 7354 0777
www.fatfacedcat.com
Wed, Fri, Sat 10–6pm
Sun 11–5pm

Angel . **Vinatge**

Charming and eccentric, this quiet shop on genteel Georgian Amwell Street might have been here for a long long time. Daylight creeps through the silk scarves in the window to reveal fabric patching on the care-worn floorboards. Shoes, bags and accessories are presented in cabinets that belong to another era. Those romantic souls who hanker for tactile engagement with a more feminine age will love the soft leather bags that are the mainstay of **Lie down i think i love you**. Selling as a label since 2006, the shop came into being in 2009 to allow the designers to offer their product in a much more personal fashion. Clients are invited to consult with them to create a bespoke bag, choosing a vintage scarf from the designers' hand-picked selection to co-ordinate with their preferred shade of leather. Beautiful print shoes and sweet dresses can also be bought in-store. *GT*

MAP 16 Ref. 6
Lie down i think i love you
33 Amwell Street
Islington EC1R 1UR
+44 (0)20 7833 1100
www.liedownithinkiloveyou.com
Mon–Fri 10–6pm

It's not just knitters who respond to the warmth, colour and softness of the yarns at **Loop**. With the variety numbering over 100, from all around the globe, it's boggling to behold the 8ply Mongolian cashmere, organic merino, Peruvian alpaca, Japanese bamboo yarn, silk, llama fibre and the many possibilities of cotton. More uncommon blends such as silk covered steel will specifically appeal to weavers and jewellery makers. Divided across a wall of cubby holes, the skeins form a kaleidescopic backdrop to the upstairs lounge which is arranged with easy chairs for anyone wishing to drop in with their knitting. This is where they hold the great SOS sessions, with tea and cake, for help with those tricky stitches, as well as a plethora of other classes. Late night openings allow for leisurely perusal of textile themed gifts such as textured ceramics, jewellery and mixed media artwork. *GT*

MAP 17 Ref. 9

Loop
15 Camden Passage
Islington N1 8EA
+44 (0)20 7288 1160
www.loopknitting.com
Tue–Sat 11–6pm
except Thu 11–7.30pm
Sun 12–5pm

Angel . **Crafts**

Pennies

Yearn for the days when women were adorned with feathers and fur rather than nylon? Yearn no more. **Pennies** is your spiritual home. Evangelical about all things vintage they sell an exquisite selection of bridal and party wear from the 20s onwards alongside antiques and jewelry that recall a time when women carried handkerchiefs, men carried snuff boxes and a second plate under your teacup was considered de rigeur. Flapper dresses and bolero jackets line the walls and nighties, wedding and prom dresses fill the rails.

Owner Penny's son Oliver is a sartorial archaeologist scouring auctions, fairs and sites to find high-quality pieces which they can repair and re-bead to retain the integrity of the original (down to sourcing original beads and learning lapsed techniques). No bigger than a boudoir and smelling like a powderpuff there are some museum-quality pieces here and also affordable accessories for the glamour-starved. *TT*

MAP 16 Ref. 7

Pennies
41a Amwell Street
Islington EC1R 1UR
+44 (0)20 7278 3827
www.penniesvintage.com
Tues–Fri 11–7pm
Sat 11–5pm
Or by appointment

Discount*

Smug is probably how you'd feel if you lived in this dinky duplex. With its raised ground floor window overlooking Camden Passage, this lifestyle shop feels more like a comfortable apartment than a centre of commerce. The kitchen-themed area downstairs and upper level reception room have on offer everything required to kit out a bijou home almost entirely, albeit one that displays a taste for formica bordering on the fetishistic. From retro furniture, through illustrated cushions and vibrant kitchen utensils to cute jewellery and the make-up on your dressing table, it's all been thought of. Visitors with a taste for life's finer things will notice the original artwork throughout. Selected by the people behind the Lodeveans Collection, whose influence was instrumental in bringing the works of Tracey Emin et al to public acclaim, unique pieces cost between £200 and £500. A modest sum for your first share of the contemporary art market. *GT*

MAP 17 Ref. 8

Smug

13 Camden Passage

Islington N1 8EA

+44 (0)20 7354 0253

www.ifeelsmug.com

Wed, Fri, Sat 11–6pm

Thu 12–7pm

Sun 12–5pm

Angel . **Home**

A working textile design studio, this tiny shop on a corner of Amwell Street is merely the tip of an iceberg. Downstairs, beneath the pavement, is where **Wallace & Sewell** create woven designs that sell throughout the world. In the UK they can be found in shops at Tate and the British Museum as well as fashion stores. Their style is distinctive in its bold use of colour with geometric patterns worked out in wool, silk, cashmere, linen and cotton chenille. Designs available here include throws, cushions and scarves that haven't been produced for wholesale as well as pieces from earlier collections. Scarves are typically produced in runs of 25 to 50 making them fairly exclusive at prices between £40 and £140. Far more ubiquitous are their upholstery designs. From 2011 the London Tube's Central line seats will also be the proud bearers of the Wallace Sewell style. *GT*

MAP 16 Ref. 5

Wallace & Sewell
24 Lloyd Baker Street
Islington WC1X 9AZ
+44 (0)20 7833 2995
www.wallacesewell.com
Tue–Fri 10.30–5.30pm
Sat 11–6pm

The deluxe ambiance of this particular **Workshop** could be misconstrued. Witness the early customers to Islington's latest fashion house who discovered to their delight that Italian quality can deliver a far lighter blow to the purse than expected. The concept at Workshop is as simple as its designs. To offer an enduring Italian elegance to London. Their range of unstructured dresses, coats and jackets in a signature fabric of boiled wool knitwear that has the semblance of felt is definitely not mass market. Designed by a London-based Italian and produced in Italy these are highly covetable garments to flatter an age range of twenty-five and beyond. Colours are muted and the silhouettes serene. Although predominantly for women, Workshop also produces men's wool jackets in the same well-tailored fashion. *GT*

MAP 17 Ref. 10

Workshop
19 Camden Passage
Islington N1 8EA
+44 (0)20 7226 3141
www.workshop-london.com
Mon–Sun 11–7pm

Angel . **Fashion**

Bagman & Robin a.k.a. Marco and Lee design highly individual leather and fabric bags. This dynamic duo operate out of a tiny atelier at the back of an equally dinky shop where they also sell Lee's paintings and prints – roosters and goldfish being an enduringly colourful theme. The bags are a mix of svelte evening clutches and capacious day bags. Marco trained as a mechanical engineer specialising in thermo-dynamics. While his bags won't make you go faster, they've been engineered to last and are finely-turned with loving attention to detail. Working from a palette of matt and glossy leathers with embossed sections and incorporating fabric from vintage Italian fashion or Japanese kimonos each bag is practically unique with no more than 3 likely to be made in any one fabric and fewer than 15 in any particular style. Large day bags cost between £150 and £180 with the more petite starting at £40. _GT_

MAP 16 Ref. 3
Bagman & Robin
47 Exmouth Market
Islington EC1R 4QL
+44 (0)20 7833 8780
www.bagmanandrobin.com
Mon–Sat 11–6pm

Brill recalls the cafés of Melbourne in its carefree and conversational approach. The tables, street-side are always taken. Specials (bagel combos, bowls of salad, 'any combination just ask') are marked up on a chalkboard and the countertop is a convivial selection of local baked goods, weekend baklava (£1) and bagels from Brick Lane (the owner Jeremy picks them up on his way in). But don't be fooled by the casual ethic. There are two things Brill are deadly serious about – music and coffee. Jeremy

Brill ran a record shop, the beloved Clerkenwell Music RIP, on this site for years and the slim but select CDs that today line the walls have been distilled down by his industry knowhow and familiarity of his customer base. You're in safe hands. Ditto the coffee. It's pedigree is local (London's Union coffee) but its execution is pure Australia, 'where the good coffee is'. Flat whites are things of beauty. And us natives are now totally addicted. Poor saps. *TT*

MAP 16 Ref. 2

Brill
27 Exmouth market
Islington EC1R 4QL
+44 (0)20 7833 9757
www.clerkenwellmusic.co.uk
Mon–Fri 10.30–6.30pm
Sat 10.30–5.30pm

Free coffee on purchase over £20 on CDs*

The Triple Bottom Line, in corporate-speak, means that you consider the planet as well as profit and people when running your business. They could have been talking about **Family Tree**. Its owners have quietly sourced stock that is either fairtrade, ethical or from small designer makers (often local) and with this they furnish their ticklish-of-spirit and strong-of-design shop. Nothing smacks of overt ethics. Smart, i-phone compatible gloves (£27 in racing green and turquoise) and Groupes leather handlebar grips,

displayed antler-like on the wall, show a flair for en vogue while handmade gifts – sake cups by Ikuko Iwamoto (£20) and papercraft cards from product designer Sato Hisao (from £2) have the hallmarks of a keen designer's eye (the owners are graphic designers both). Family Tree's own line - lighting, furniture and jewelry with designs taken from Kimono fabrics – are beautiful and deservedly well known. As should this small but important shop be. TT

MAP 16 Ref. 4

Family Tree
53 Exmouth Market
Ec1R 4QL
+44 (0)20 7278 1084
www.familytreeshop.co.uk
Mon–Sat 11–6pm

Aptly located at the turn into Spa Fields is **The Klinik** hairdressing salon. While clinically white in appearance, any sense of austerity is melted by the warmth of the welcome from this international team of stylists. Helmed by Swedish owner Anna there's no salon hierarchy, everyone here being equally qualified and performing the same tasks. This, along with the neutral and unintimidating interior, might explain why nearly half the client base is men. Or is it something to do with those cameras? A monitor at each seat allows the customer to see precisely what's happening to their locks. Designed to empower the patron, it's a mesmerising tool. Ever forward-looking, new products at the klinik include the sulphate, paraben and gluten-free *Unite* range, 100% ammonia-free colours by *L'Oréal* and a non-permanent Brazilian keratin treatment for smoothing frizzy hair that lasts for up to 4 months. *GT*

MAP 16 Ref. 1
The Klinik
28 Exmouth Market
Islington EC1R 4QE
+44 (0)20 7837 3771
www.theklinik.com
Mon–Fri 9–8pm
Sat 9–5pm

The Klinik

The Primrose Hill set love this eccentric store. Owner **Daniel Poole** – best known for his bold and industrial nineties streetwear – draws on his love for avant garde design to curate an incredible space filled with curios and a constantly morphing cornucopia of peculiar found objects, made furniture, artworks and antiques. Snoopers will love eyeing up shelves packed with old toys, lighting and vintage ephemera, while those looking to invest in a larger piece will enjoy rock 'n' roll sofas and one-off furniture items. The store also hosts a changing display of art and past exhibitions have included witty neon signage by artist Chris Bracey and homeware design by Rory Dobner – perfect retail fodder for the area's creative types with a weakness for the unique. ZA.

MAP 18 Ref. 23

Daniel Poole

156 Regents Park Road

Primrose Hill NW1 8XL

www.danielpoole.com

Tues–Sun 10–6pm

Its air thick with Wild Fig and Grape (courtesy of the shop's own candles), **Judith Michael & Daughter** is a vintage treasure trove offering shiny campness as well as retro cool. Mirrored Art Deco furniture and costume jewellery (including some made for the Suffragettes) keep the magpies happy, while 1950s Playboy magazines, Japanese fortune-telling cups and Brazilian voodoo dolls satisfy more quirky gift-buyers. Owner Gillian Anderson Price is one of the interiors experts on ITV's House Gift, and her keen eye sets the shop apart from identikit emporiums. The old is sprinkled with the new: Keep Calm And Carry On signs fit right in with vintage Union Jack cushions; Victorian Champagne saucers are accompanied by 'Harlequin' cutlery. Boasts Jude Law, Sadie Frost and Kate Moss as clients – but then so do most of our other Primrose Hill picks. *FM*

MAP 18 Ref. 21

Judith Michael & Daughter
73 Regents Park Road
Primrose Hill NW1 8UY
+44 (0)20 7722 9000
www.judithmichael.com
Mon–Sat 10–6pm
Sun 12–6pm

Its shelves heaving with wasabi, pickled ginger and wakame and its floor taken up by a rowing boat filled with ice and the latest catch, **La Petite Poissonerie** is not your average fishmonger. French owner Nic Rascle, a trained chef, is so keen to espouse the wonders of gilled creatures that he's building a swanky kitchen downstairs to host classes ranging from sushi-making and filleting to longer sessions taking in lobster and foie gras (prices will start at £35 per person). 'I hope to create a lunchtime hour where people can come and learn a few dishes – such as moules marinieres, Thai and Spanish mussels cooked by competing teams – and then eat them with some wine,' he says, excitedly describing the herb garden he's planning to plant outside, with rosemary, thyme and lavender. Customers can wander around the boat to pick their fish of the day, or even take home some sushi-grade wares to eat raw. *FM*

MAP 18 Ref. 24

La Petite Poissonerie
75 Gloucester Avenue
Primrose Hill NW1 8LD
+44 (0)20 7483 4435
www.lapetitepoissonerie.com
Tues–Sat 9.30–7.30pm
Sun 10.30–5.30pm

Primrose Bakery

Primrose Hill could lay claim to being one of London's most fervent defenders of independents, as residents successfully blocked a Starbucks eight years ago, the first time the chain had been forced to back down. **Primrose Bakery** couldn't be further from the ubiquitous coffee purveyor, offering a warm, icing sugar-scented haven for locals and tourists to sit for hours. So popular that it attracts a queue worthy of a late-night kebab shop, synonymous with the recent cupcake revival (its first recipe book was a bestseller, and a second book is due out next year). After baking cupcakes for their children's birthday parties, two local mothers began supplying to deli Melrose and Morgan in 2004. They now supply Selfridges, Liberty and Fortnum & Mason, and a second Primrose Bakery opened in Covent Garden 18 months ago. The original has a reassuringly homemade feel, bunting and 1950s chairs offering a cosy setting for customers wanting tea and crumpets as well as cupcakes with flavours such as Earl Grey, peanut butter, rose and coconut. *FM*

MAP 18 Ref. 25

Primrose Bakery
69 Gloucester Avenue
Primrose Hill NW1 8LD
+44 (0)20 7483 4222
www.primrosebakery.org.uk
Mon–Sat 8.30–6pm
Sun 10–5pm

Shika Suki

Set up in 2004 by Central St Martins graduate Rachel Ducker, **Shika Suki** is more museum than shop. Every item has been lovingly tagged and arranged in a way that is curated rather than merely displayed, from the selection of vintage bisque Nancy Ann dolls in the corner to the wall of chiffon squares and silk scarves. Japan meets Portobello with Technicolor childrens' accessories, including vintage Dream Pets and Barbie cases, alongside shelves of neatly placed metal belts and owl necklaces. Quotes from Alice Temperley and Matthew Williamson on the shop's website attest to its fashion credentials, confirmed by a collection of Ossie Clark dresses. But it's the racks downstairs that set it apart: colour-coordinated cocktail dresses, beaded cardigans and bucket bags provide the range of Rokit without the feeling of ploughing through a car boot sale. *FM*

MAP 18 Ref. 26

Shika Suki
67 Gloucester Avenue
Primrose Hill NW1 8LD
+44 (0)20 7722 4442
www.shikasuki.com
Mon–Sun 11–7pm

The best independent shops have their own smells, and **Studio 8**'s scent speaks of old leather and the finer things in life. There's plenty of that for sale here – Italian label Calabrese's Pantcuoi slippers, with leather uppers and crepe soles, mingle with Barbour jackets and vintage watches (owner Simon Savage has just started selling these online, his passion for them inspired by his deep-sea diver father). Yet luxury brands mix with edgier designers to create a style that's a little bit Bond Street, a little bit Brick Lane.

So a two-grand Heuer is joined by Timex multicoloured digital watches at £25 a pop, and Comme des Garcons loafers sit alongside £39 tennis shoes by Supergra. Womens labels include Acne, Ash and Rick Owens, and staff are so attentive they keep aside items they think regulars might like. A definite one-off. *FD*

MAP 18 Ref. 22
Studio 8
83 Regents Park Road
Primrose Hill NW1 8UY
+44 (0)20 7449 0616
www.studio8shop.com
Mon–Sat 10–6pm
Except Thu 10–7pm
Sun 12–5pm

Primrose Hill . *Fashion*

Like a delightfully disordered jewellery box, **Bones** is stuffed to the gills with things to adorn, embellish and tickle. Ceilings sparkle with candelabras, Moorish lamps and winking fairy lights while dressers groan with mirrors, frames and ceramics. Stock is modern-to-look vintage and rummaging is thoroughly recommended. Once the eye stills there are some quite solid furniture pieces anchoring the stock – large wooden chests with good tongue and groove joining – and Bones can order in larger items from their collection of catalogues. Quirky home-ware accessories are what they are beloved for, like a recession-friendly PIP china set starting from £9.50 (pastel palette, oriental print). The staff know their market and their clients and are impassioned members of the Traders Association, championing Independent shops' right, nay, duty to be different. Of which Bones is an eloquent, eccentric ambassador. *TT*

MAP 20 Ref. 32
Bones
253 Muswell Hill Broadway
Muswell Hill N10 1DE
+44 (0)20 8883 4730
www.bonesfurniture.co.uk
Mon–Sat 9.30–6pm
Sun 12–5pm

-10%

Discount on items over £50*

Cha-Cha-Cha puts the eek! into weekend. School girls exclaim over Christian Dior sunglasses from the 70s (£65) and buyers from Hennes and Accessorize come to copy designs for their lines. There is not a bum note among the stock but the real find are the staff, sartorially passionate and with an encyclopaedic knowledge of their (four) rails. Use them. With their help we paired a red carpet, black vintage silk gown with hooks and eyes and a bustle (£100) with a 40s-ration inspired bolero jacket (£45) for less than the price of a Pringles skirt. Brides can beat the recession (£25 wedding dress) and old dresses need never die (Megan Stevenson upcycles old curtains/vintage dress material for her bespoke lampshades). Online there is furniture too but the real alchemy is in the attic to 30s jive and playful encouragement. TT

MAP 20 Ref. 33
Cha-Cha-Cha
20-22 Avenue Mews
Muswell Hill N10 3NP
+44 (0)773951 7855
+44 (0)7974 043616
www.cha-cha-cha.co.uk
Fri–Sat 11–5pm
Sun 12–5pm

Café doesn't do this justice. It is a destination point. – **Emporium Teas** is a nostalgic hijack. A community cornerstone. Run as a social enterprise supporting TreeHouse School pupils into work experience, it is by definition local. Everything hails from near here, from the art on the wall to the staff and regulars, to the tea on the trolley (from the excellent, nearby W Martyn). During the day it hums with the smell of fresh baking and bustling custom. Tables are square and pretty, walls are hung with the current 'On the Wall' seasonal art. Menus are pretension-free – porridge and golden syrup, toast and homemade marmalade, specials show a seasonal flair and their Afternoon Tea (a heaving cake stand of fingersandwiches, brownies and cakes plus tea, £14 each, book 24 hours in advance) is the stuff of legend and weightgain. TT

MAP 20 Ref. 39
Emporium Tea Rooms
4/5 Cheapside
Fortis Green
Muswell Hill N2 9HP
+44 (0)20 8883 8098
www.emporiumtearooms.co.uk
Mon–Sat 9–5pm

There is a lot of superfluous baby 'stuff' out there. Happily, the ethos and space constraints at **O Baby** means they have whittled down your options to a few, choice, scrupulously sourced, ethical necessities (real nappies, potties, slings, washes, sleepbags, Sophie giraffes etc.) plus a beautiful clothing line and small but perfectly formed selection of traditional toys. Scandinavian in look and feel (stripped wooden shelves/floors, recessed lighting) O Baby is a resolutely customer-geared experience – a basket of toys on the floor, an unseen toilet out back, and 'Fancy a game of netball?' request on the cash till. Clothing lines - Green Baby, Minymo, Ej Sikke Lej, Littlechook, Piccalilly - are unusual and covetable, Fairtrade and 80 per cent organic. And toys (a DIY cardboard house) encourage imagination rather than passive button pushing. Expect heavy through-traffic from loyal, locals where this is, deservedly, a byword in trust and good taste. *TT*

MAP 20 Ref. 37
O Baby
126 Fortis Green Road
Muswell Hill N10 3DU
+44 (0)20 8444 8742
Mon–Sat 9.30–5.30pm

If only there was one shop where girls could buy everything they need to complete their wardrobe, well I think we've found it! **Rossandco** cover everything and stylishly too. We're talking one place where you can buy daywear; smart and casual dresses and trousers, alongside cosy knitwear, sumptuous evening dresses and delicate clutch bags. And it doesn't stop there, they have a great range of quirky jewellery and accessories, all hand selected which make great gifts and lovely cut glass and mirrored jewellery boxes and of course no elegant shop is complete without posh candles. Whether you need a silk scarf, a retro umbrella or a fun pair of shoes this excellent selection will ensure women of all ages will find something perfect. *PB*

MAP 20 Ref. 34

Rossandco

152 Muswell Hill Broadway

Muswell Hill N10 3SA

+44 (0)20 8883 9122

FB rossandco

Mon–Sat 10–6pm

Sun 12–5pm

The first thing that comes to mind here is that the **Rosie Brown Boutique** is definitely the product of someone who likes to shop for a living, how else would it be filled with so many quirky and pretty things? There are lovely fabric covered notebooks, colourful tins and purses, picture frames and clothes. Rosie Brown knows her customers and likes to provide things for women of all ages whether it's a cosy cardigan or fun bits and pieces for the kitchen. Perfect for gifts, it's the kind of shop you pop in to buy a nice cushion or silk scarf and end up buying a bronze frog, beaded coat hanger or some more candle holders for the bathroom, in other words you'll walk out with more presents for yourself than the intended recipient. *PB*

MAP 20 Ref. 38

Rosie Brown Boutique
224-228 Fortis Green Road
Muswell Hill N10 3DU
+44 (0)20 8883 5385
www.rosiebrownonthemove.com
Mon–Sat 10.15–6pm
Sun 12–5pm

-15%

Discount*

Sally Bourne Interiors cater to everything 'home' from the paint on your walls and curtain swag to tiling, blinds, the earthenware in your cupboard and candles on the sideboard. The heaps of inspirational fabric swatch books to order from and a made to measure service for curtains and blinds detail the shop's 'working' nature with a central dias for fabric cutting and tile and paint stations. Bourne's hugely knowledgeable staff can navigate you through all their 12,000 shades of Farrow&Ball, Designers Guild, Sanderson's paints and a comprehensive consultancy service is available for more advanced interior aid. This is more than off the peg designer application - genuine creativity abounds. Ribbon spools are displayed in aluminium guttering, card stock is kept in wooden crates and wallpaper rolls hang from custom-made, Shaker-inspired coat pegs. The shop's signature style is evident everywhere from the visionary window displays to beautiful bundles of kindling (£3.99). I'm tempted. And I don't even own a fire. *TT*

MAP 20 Ref. 35

Sally Bourne Interiors
26 The Broadway
Muswell Hill N10 3RT
+44 (0)20 8444 3031
www.sallybourneinteriors.co.uk
Mon–Sat 10–6pm
Sun 12–5pm (mid Oct–Dec)

Second Nature feels thematic, like a museum. Although its contents can loosely be described as garden ephemera – flowers, planters, candles, container solutions - you navigate it like a visitor; reverential, respectful; here a family of sepia prints, a 'butterfly corner' (notebooks, desk calendars, specimens), there, a Wellington-fronted egg collector cabinet with replica eggs. There is a taxonomist's touch to everything – stuff collected, catalogued then lost again to the jumble of competing items from gardeners

kneelers to first edition Penguin prints (£14). Everything is either beautiful, old or useful. Often all three. Orchids grow from vintage tea caddies. Brown paper Heritage Seeds (£2 each) sit in sifting trays. Up on a peg a Rectory folding chair makes a makeshift store for candles, bubble-bath, soaps. It smells of clove oil and the seasonal flowers Parker makes up in arrangements as bespoke and beautiful as the tiny space he so joyously curates. *TT*

MAP 20 Ref. 36
Second Nature
79 Fortis Green Road
Muswell Hill N10 3HP
+44 (0)20 8444 1717
Tue–Sat 9–6pm
Sun–Mon 11–4.30pm

Muswell Hill . *Plants*

You know when you start selling name-brand jute bags that you have graduated from being a venue to a brand; a by-word for relaxation. **The Haberdashery** inspires a lifestyle loyalty from its clientèle. From the mismatched furniture and hot drinks in jam jars, to a scratchy vinyl soundtrack it leaves the polish and perfection to Starbucks and instead gives permission to unwind. Actors and creatives huddle in the high vaulted cafe (strung-bunting, fairy lights, pretty folding chairs) or the cobbled yard out back fuelled by home-baked pastries (polenta bread in terracotta pots) and Massimo's rocket-fuel (all the coffee is by Bristot - a small niche coffee maker from northern Italy). At night the cafe becomes an intimate venue for parties/weddings/ bazaars and exhibitions with a full liquor license (cocktails in vintage china cups) and wait-staff who recall Vincent Gallo in candy-striped aprons. The spirit of early New York, in N8. *TT*

MAP 19 Ref. 31
The Haberdashery
22 Middle Lane
Crouch End N8 8PL
+44 (0)20 8342 8098
www.the-haberdashery.com
Mon–Fri 8–6pm
Sat–Sun 9–6pm

Shakespeare may have counselled putting away childish things but **Indish** springs the toy chest to revive that essence of childhood – play, colour, invention – and make it a requisite for their resolutely grown up, designer stock. This small Crouch End institution has, for 15 years, been bringing colour to the burbs courtesy of Marimekko napkins, ISAK lovebird cups (£9.50) and MAGIS brooms in bold, primary hues. A shop of giftware, domestic designer-ware (Flos, Kartell, Pigeon lighting, an £80 Jacob Jenson

smoke alarm anyone?) and visual punditry (the Bookrest Lamp and Thelermont Hupton's hang-loose coat-hook) its stock changes seasonally and is designed to tickle its punters and accommodate every pocket be that a Magis Deja-vu table by Naoto Fukasawa (£1,115) or a £2.50 Japanese panda paper balloon. *TT*

MAP 19 Ref. 28
Indish
16 Broadway Parade
Crouch End N8 9DE
+44 (0)20 8340 1188
www.indish.co.uk
Mon–Sat 10.30–5.30pm
Sun 12.30–4.30pm

Little Paris

Ever spent lazy afternoons rummaging through the French Brocante markets? Us neither. But lucky for us **Little Paris**' owners do, regularly, and recreate a fiction immeasurably more beautiful than actual fact. Owner Helene Allen wanted to make a space that embodied the spirit of her homeland and she succeeds. Accessories - leather handbags and silk scarves by young designers that she follows avidly and buys modestly (one, maybe two to keep her lines exclusive) – recall the street stalls of the Left Bank while the rest of the shop evokes a rambling, rural market. Pieces range from substantial-to-small – burnished industrial drawers (£950), a cow garden statue (£130) and vintage advertising posters (£10) for those of us without a chateau to refurbish. Weekends attract bargain-hungry Brits and French expatriates who congregate here informally – visibly relaxing amongst all that beauty. *TT*

MAP 19 Ref. 30

Little Paris
39 Park Road
Crouch End N8 8TE
+44 (0)20 8340 9008
www.littleparis.co.uk
Mon 11–6pm
Tue–Fri 10–6pm
Sat 10.30–6pm
Sun 11–5pm

-10%
Discount*

Quite possibly the best ice cream shop for those out there who consider eating ice cream too much of an indulgence, **Riley** have a remarkable selection of sorbets so creamy and delicious in flavours like chocolate and blood orange, you'll think you're eating ice cream! Not only that, they serve coffee, delicious cakes and a lunch buffet too. Opened by two friends, one with a love of ice cream and the other with considerable knowledge in the food industry, they went all out, getting expert teaching from a master ice cream maker from Bologna. The ice cream and sorbet is made below the shop which gives them the opportunity to experiment with flavours, such as pumpkin, (which apparently didn't work), and pink grapefruit which was a winner. *PB*

MAP 19 Ref. 27

Riley
32 The Broadway
Crouch End N8 9SU
+44 (0)20 83477825
Mon–Sun 9–5pm

Sable d'Or

Sable d'Or Patisserie recalls the opening frames of Chocolat – the curved frontage, the marbled counter tops, the little confectionary creations in their paper casing cuffs. Inside it smells of fresh ground coffee and melted butter from the baking that happens here daily (chocolate gateaux, cheesecakes, butter croissants). Pretty waitresses ferry cleansing juices (at a very reasonable £2.50) and breakfast orders of crepes, brioches, open sandwiches between two well proportioned rooms and small tables that inspire intimate clinches and a low, respectful hubub. The atmosphere is continental, convivial, unhurried and, like it's sister shop in Muswell Hill, it shares a signature look of whitewashed walls, exposed brickwork, tiled floors and artwork by local talent. Cold drinks are top quality – Pukka, Chegworth Valley, James White – and the coffee is frothy and transporting. *TT*

MAP 19 Ref. 29
Sable d' Or
43 The Broadway
Crouch End N8 8DT
+44 (0)20 8341 7789
Mon–Sun 8–6pm

There is a gentlemen's agreement among independent stores that to stock that which your neighbour stocks, is simply not cricket. This could be a problem for **Homage**, joining as it does the thrum of other homewares shops on Church St but happily they have a playful take on interiors which is unlikely to suffer duplication. Duck coat hook? Old drum recliner? You get the picture. Homage's USP, if it has such a thing, is the uplift of old, beautiful things (reupholstered, recycled, restored) and an accent of new, beautiful things. Upstairs cups, plates, pots and lampshades are displayed simply in wooden apple crates. Downstairs large pieces by industrial revivalists Otentic partner prints, pillows and furnishings by playful, new designers. Owners Mark and Liza are recent exiles from the world of large-scale, retail buying and their evident excitement for the small-scale, the authentic and the eccentric quite literally colours this shop. TT

MAP 21 Ref. 45

Homage

106 Stoke Newington Church St

N16 0LA

+44 (0)20 3556 8362

www.homageonline.co.uk

Tues–Sat 11–6pm

Sun 12–5pm

-10%

Offer ends 31st Jan 2012 *

Stoke Newington. *Home*

243

Hub has two clothing outlets, each with its own distinctive character, within shouting distance of one another. To the north is the reassuringly old-fashioned men's shop. The appearance of a gentlemen's outfitters is consistent with the service: unobtrusive but available for those who require it. Clothes for the urbane but rugged man about town are well-made, of fine fabric and this lady writer could happily spend all day there, running her hands over the orderly piles of denim and woollens. The women's shop is equally welcoming and easy to navigate. Both have a mix of solid everyday staples – *Lee, Acne* and *Dr Denim* – punctuated by the eye-catching, such as *Something Else* for women and *Jacey Withers* jewellery for men. There's a British-made bias which includes Hub's own labels *Yarn* and *Beth Graham*. Producing as few as ten of any one item makes these pieces exclusively good value. *GT*

MAP 21 Ref. 42

Hub
49 Stoke Newington
Church Street
Stoke Newington N16 0AP
+44 (0)20 7254 4494
www.hubshop.co.uk
Mon–Sat 10.30–6.30pm
Sun 11–5pm

Ladies, men's and children's shoes, all under one roof, on one floor and well-displayed in a light and airy showroom. Almost unbelievable. But here it is. The spread of brands encompasses practical to quirky, and many are both. Predominantly European, many British and with an occasional highlight from the U.S., this selection shows a fascination for design that permeates the store. As with many independents, **Mudfoot & Scruff** is a family business that grew from the owners' own needs and what they felt to be lacking in their local marketplace. It's a tranquil, welcoming and comfortable space with a spare interior that makes for easy browsing, showing off the footwear to its best advantage. If your need for comfort, craftsmanship and good materials equals your passion for style, you'll appreciate the many obscure as well as familiar names including Dutch label Grotesque and new Brits on the block Rakish Heels and Esska. *GT*

MAP 21 Ref. 48
Mudfoot & Scruff
166 Stoke Newington
Church Street
Stoke Newington N16 0JL
+44 (0)20 7241 3009
Mon–Sat 11–6pm
Sun 11–5pm

Quietly out of the way, **Of Cabbages & Kings** is tucked around the corner from the well-trodden Church Street. Its appearance as gift shop belies its true identity of craft and art gallery. Fine art prints by local illustrators make up the core of its stock, mostly in limited editions. As is often the case with designers who aren't producing for a mass-market, the work is all the more appealing for being so individual and undiluted in style. Unusual jewellery and ceramics are likewise often produced locally and in small numbers, making them exclusive despite the competitive pricing. With so many designer-makers in the area, a monthly market in nearby Abney Hall has been set up to accommodate the overspill from the shop. See Of *Cabbages & Kings*' website for dates. For particular presents and distinctive objects for the home, it's well worth a deviation from the main drag. *GT*

MAP 21 Ref. 43

Of Cabbages & Kings
34b Kersley Road
Stoke Newington N16 0NH
+44 (0)20 7254 0060
www.ofcabbages.co.uk
Tue–Sat 11–6pm
Sun 1–5pm

Olive Loves Alfie isn't just clothes for kids. A visit for children's things is as likely to result in a new dress by *Marimekko* or all the christmas shopping in one fell swoop. Owner Ashlyn is not a fan of throw-away culture so everything is chosen with hand-me-down potential in mind. Many of the labels stocked use organic cotton – see *Monkey Genes* and the often entertaining *Mini-Rodini* – others are Fairtrade. The minefield of provenance has been picked through by Ashlyn and she can answer queries on these details. Beautifully illustrated books on wildlife and nature reflect a keen sense of aesthetics and make sense in a shop full of fun camping accessories. Nearly everything can be purchased via the comprehensive and inspiring website but a visit is a treat, if only to appreciate the variety of child-focused original artwork available to commission, great for those extra-special gifts. *GT*

MAP 21 Ref. 44
Olive Loves Alfie
84 Stoke Newington
Church Street
Stoke Newington N16 0AP
+44 (0)20 7241 4212
www.olivelovesalfie.co.uk
Mon–Fri 9.30–5.30pm
Sat 10–6pm
Sun 12–5pm

Many pictures. Fewer lights. Quite a lot of ceramics. Some glassware and a fair smattering of delicate jewellery. All very organised. Tidy. And neat. From among a stack of prints, one in particular calls for attention, its letters pressed in grainy woodblock type. Says William Morris "Have nothing in your home that you do not know to be useful, or believe to be beautiful". And there is the summation of things at **Pictures & Light**. If it's not one, it's the other. Specifically, lights are from the 1960s and '70s and cost up to £150. Pictures, or rather prints, are mostly Czech or Spanish language posters – vintage graphics, cherry-picked for their chalky colours and bold words. Most wonderful are the framed sheets culled from music scores, film journals and technical manuals of the last century. Never before has *Practical Wireless* seemed so beautiful. *GT*

MAP 21 Ref. 41
Pictures & Light
41 Stoke Newington
Church Street
Stoke Newington N16 0NX
+44 (0)20 7923 7923
Thu–Sun 11–6pm

Rouge offers a joyful splash of colour on an otherwise pallid English pavement. Owner Lei, a design graduate of Kingston University, is from Beijing and her buying ethos favours vivid hues and handicraft. She sources homewares, furniture and accessories from Japan, Vietnam and Thailand but predominantly rural China where she pursues the dwindling stock of reclaimed and reconditioned rustic furniture which dominates her range. As such she can advise customers on origins or suggest new pieces made from sustainably sourced wood. Aside from the painted wardrobes and chests is an array of delicate ceramics, hand-painted cards and ephemera, origami sets, automata and children's fabric bootees, toys and animals featuring appliqué and embroidery designs. The selection is noticeably different to anything on offer in Chinatown and has been chosen with the modern European home in mind, there being also a sister shop in central Brussels. *GT*

MAP 21 Ref. 40

Rouge
158 Stoke Newington
High Street
Stoke Newington N16 7JL
+44 (0)20 7275 0887
www.rouge-shop.co.uk
Mon–Sat 11–6.30pm
closed on Tue
Sun 12–5pm

-5%

Discount*

Yes, that name is plural. Not one, but two, exceedingly big rooms. Further tables in the garden only add to the relaxing space of these traditional **Tea Rooms**. Clientele clearly enjoy the old-fashioned set-up and the conversations that accompany the chink of china are always gentle. Pâtissière Isabelle Alfrey believes afternoon tea is a treat, and as such won't scrimp on quality or quantity. Her cake-stands heave with all manner of fruit, chocolate and nut permutations and the companion brew, chosen from a list of 20 or so teas featuring Darjeeling and Pu-erh, should refresh the most jaded palate. Meanwhile, a wandering eye can feast on the huge range of Poole pottery, collected by her mum, a published expert on the subject. Leaving without a memento isn't really an option. Those who resist the china, will most likely fall at the final hurdle of house jams, loose-leaf teas and crumbling fudge. *GT*

MAP 21 Ref. 47

The Tea Rooms
153–155 Stoke Newington
Church Street
Stoke Newington N16 0UH
+44 (0)20 7923 1870
www.thetearooms.org
Tue–Fri 11–6pm
Sat–Sun 11–6.30pm

Tin-Tone creator Jon Free makes 'sonic fascinators'; be that a 9V micro-amp build in a vintage tin (£75), a double bass made from a steamer cabin trunk or a £7.50 bottleneck 'slide' to use for guitars. He is music's Heath Robinson and his workshop-cum-home on Church Street is where he fixes guitars, sells strings and imagines new musical mutations (when he's not got highly exacting guitar repair jobs on from places like Rose Morris or Macaris. Or is fixing some school kid's broke cello).

Filled to the rafters with nuts, bolts and his handmade guitars ranging from £150 for an Old-Master 3 string Tin-Tone to £1200 for a customised, vintage guitar he sits, hot-rodding homeware and making music. *TT*

(tin·tone [tin-tohn] noun-a stringed musical instrument with a long, fretted neck made out of (typically) a table leg and a biscuit tin/lunch box for a 'resonator'. Music from 3,4 or 5 strings reverberates through a tea strainer or possibly bath plug, depending, for a sound reminiscent of the tinny, pick-y cigar-box guitars of the 1900s. Beloved by greats such as Seasick Steve, Mick Harvey, Roger Glover and Sonic Youth.)

MAP 21 Ref. 46
Tin Tone
91 Stoke Newington Church St
Newington Green N16 0AS
+44 (0)7941 908 774
www.tin-tone.com
www.blackguitars.com
Daily by appointment

Pelicans & Parrots Black

It's hard to imagine a more stylish shop, with matt black walls, dark wood floors, huge windows, simple pine shelving and exposed light bulbs it's the perfect back drop for the quirky collection of tribal masks, expertly picked out vintage clothes and industrial style furniture. The sister shop to nearby Pelicans and Parrots, **Pelicans & Parrots Black** has a more interior and anthological theme, with antlers and Dutch portraits on the wall, antique birdcages and anatomical pictures it's inspiring to the point you want to re-create the whole thing back in your own living room, complete with stuffed peacock and colourful prints of parrots and toucans. The shop has a good turnover with new things coming in all the time ensuring a different selection of pieces with each new visit. *PB*

MAP 22 Ref. 54

Pelicans & Parrots Black
81 Stoke Newington Road
Stoke Newington N16 8AD
+44 (0)20 7249 9177
www.pelicansandparrots.com
Wed–Sat 12pm–8pm
Sun 12pm–7pm

"A bicycle shop that's a bit different" they say. We'd say they've taken the bicycle repair space from perfunctory to perfect. **Push** is a graphic designer's layout come alive. Every item is in its place, aligned to the grid. It even bears its own typeface. Such design conscious attention to fine detail is reflected throughout their selection of stock. The day-glo mainstream is relegated in preference for über-considered clothing brands such as *swrve* "urban cycling apparel" and helmets by *Yakkay* and *Bern*, all of whom value form as highly as functionality. Bikes on offer include the hand-crafted steel frames of British company *Mercian*, this being their chosen London outlet. With 3 mechanics always on duty, the priority at Push is immediate attention to service and they welcome enquiries regarding restoration of old bikes, a personal passion. *GT*

MAP 22 Ref. 55
Push
35c Newington Green
Newington Green N16 9PR
+44 (0)20 7249 1351
www.pushcycles.com
Mon–Fri 8–6pm
Sat 9–5.30pm

There's a world first in Dalston. 'A farm in a shop' with produce ranging from fish to eggs, mushrooms and salads. All produced indoors. "The **FARM:shop** is a thriving experiment in urban agriculture; sustainable, fresh, food, grown within city communities." Something & Son believe it's possible to produce and sell to consumers in exciting urban spaces inspiring city dwellers to grow their own food while rebuilding a closer relationship with food. Lately replaced with packaging and branding. Enjoy a coffee or lunch amid the burbling of the tyllapia tanks and hydroponic allotments, with as many products as possible supplied by the farm or local growers. FARM:shop is the brain child of Something & Son LLP., an eco-social design practice run by Andrew Merritt and Paul Smyth (pictured). With cities traditionally consuming productive farmland, this idea might just be a viable counter balance. Look out for the contented rooftop chickens as you pass by on the upper deck of a 30 or 56 bus. *MS*

MAP 22 Ref. 50
FARM:shop
20 Dalston Lane
Dalston E8 3AZ
+44 (0)20 3490 5124
www.farmlondon.weebly.com
Mon–Sat 11–5pm

Fee Fee La Fou HQ

Every interior design book is going to want **Fee Fee La Fou HQ** on its pages. A combined love of the circus and a fascination with fairgrounds has materialised into a shop which is nothing short of an explosion of creativity and eclectic taste, with every wall painted either a bright colour or covered in wallpaper with neon smiley faces or circus elephants. Everything is for sale from the eccentric picture frames made from kitsch toys then covered with pink paint to the 1970's fairground 'Grabber Machine' and retro furniture painted in vibrant clashing colours. Handmade cushion covers combining Hee-Man and Thomas the Tank Engine along with chandeliers stuffed with toys make Fee Fee La Fou the perfect gift shop for any friend where you know a scented candle just won't cut it. *PB*

MAP 22 Ref. 51

Fee Fee La Fou HQ
6 Bradbury Street
Dalston N16 8JN
+44 (0)20 7249 1238
www.feefeelafouenterprises.com
Mon–Sat 11am–7pm

Dalston . **Art**

-10%

Discount*

Stemming from the online magazine huhmagazine.co.uk, **Huh** decided that it made natural sense to showcase the fashion collections they write about online, to sell in a shop as well. With a sophisticated store design, a bit Scandinavian, a bit Japanese with plenty of space to see what's what, good lighting, a proper coffee machine serving coffee from renowned Caravan and simple shelves made of plywood, it's the perfect compliment to the straightforward, comfortable and good quality brands they stock such as B-store, Carhartt, Cheap Monday, Pointer, Swedish Hasbeens and Opening Ceremony. Originally started as an online bookstore they carry on the theme selling offbeat magazines and photographic publications along with quirky homewares such as skyplanters, plants that hang from the ceiling like spot lights, inspired indeed. *PB*

MAP 22 Ref. 53

Huh. Store

56 Stoke Newington Road

Dalston N16 7XB

www.huhmagazine.co.uk

Tue–Fri 12–8pm

Sat 11–8pm

Sun 12–6pm

Having collected vintage designer clothes for many years and wanting to create their own label, owners of **Storm In A Teacup** took the opportunity to open a shop as this seemed like a good platform to start. Beautifully refurbished and selling classic pieces from the likes of Chanel, Issey Miyake and Thierry Mugler they also sell a limited collection by contemporary designers such as Eley Kishimoto, the idea being that they will rotate different cutting edge designers, a nice juxtaposition against the vintage aspects of the shop. The Georgian listed shop front, spider web inspired ceiling, neon Perspex shelving and shop counter made from old railway sleepers complete with shelves full of old-fashioned jars full of sweets (also for sale) insure this is no ordinary vintage designer shop. *PB*

MAP 22 Ref. 49

Storm In A Teacup
366 Kingsland Road
Dalston E8 4DA
+44 (0)20 8127 5471
www.storminateacuplondon.com
Mon & Tues Appointment only
Wed–Sat 11–7pm
Sun 12–6pm
(May vary please check website)

Dalston . Vintage

Café : Dalston

The eponymous Tina, high priestess of Sixties sultriness, presides over all proceedings at this Dalston coffee-house that's definitely worth a slide off the track. From her gilt frame, with an eye towards the throbbing pavements of Kingsland High Street, she beckons. And they come. In defiance of the heretofore overlooked location, this is now a destination to beat towards. Sunny staff, cheerful chatter and coffee made with love. Rain or shine, **Tina, We Salute You** is a congenial corner. Fight for the marmite at the communal table. Rock up for rays at a pavement pew. Snuggle on the sofa. Perch by the glass. Goddamnit, grab a takeaway and sip it by the bike racks. Is there nothing wrong with this place? Did I mention the cakes? Lush. Homemade! And getting ever more elaborate. But hurry, because that menu changes with the wind. And the art… come see for yourself. *GT*

MAP 22 Ref. 52

Tina, We Salute You
47 King Henry's Walk
Dalston N1 4NH
+44 (0)20 3119 0047
www.tinawesaluteyou.com
Tue–Fri 8–7pm
Sat 9–7pm
Sun 10–7pm

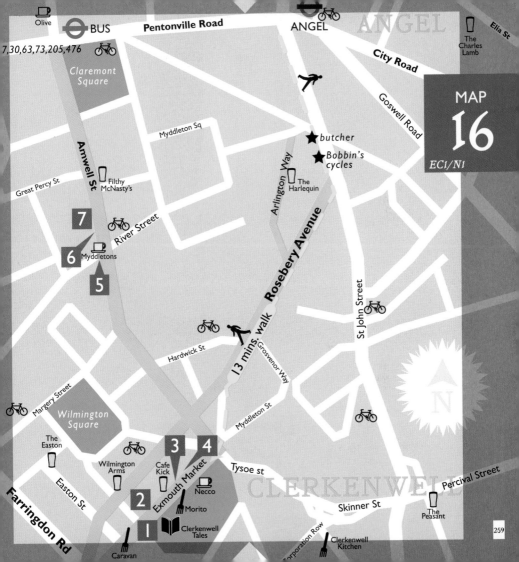

Olive

BUS

7,30,63,73,205,476

Claremont Square

Pentonville Road

ANGEL

ANGEL

City Road

The Charles Lamb

Elia St

MAP

16

EC1/N1

Goswell Road

Myddleton Sq

★ *butcher*

★ *Bobbin's cycles*

Amwell St

Great Percy St

Filthy McNasty's

River Street

The Harlequin

Arlington Way

Rosebery Avenue

7

6 Myddletons

5

St John Street

Hardwick St

13 mins. walk

Grosvenor Way

Margery Street

Wilmington Square

Myddleton St

The Easton

Wilmington Arms

3 4

Easton St

2

Exmouth Market

Cafe Kick

Necco

Tysoe st

Morito

Clerkenwell Tales

CLERKENWELL

Percival Street

Skinner St

The Peasant

1

Farringdon Rd

Caravan

Corporation Row

Clerkenwell Kitchen

MAP

17

N1

Thornhill Rd

Islington Park St

New Rose

Canonbury St

Upper St

17

⊖ BUS

43

18

19

20

Barnsbury St

ISLINGTON

16 mins. walk

16

15

14

13

12

Cross St

The Albion

The Barnsbury

The Regent

Liverpool Rd

Cross + Stitch

New Rose

fresh fish

★

Essex Rd

Saponara

The Crown

Cloudesley Rd

Theberton St

The Kings Head

Upper St

Packington St

Islington Green

Gt. Peter's St

The Mucky Pup

Barnsbury Rd

The Elk in the Woods

11

Gipfel

Charlton Pl

Colebrook Row

Grantbridge St

Duke of Cambridge

Ritchie St

9

10

Parkfield St

Camden Passage

8

Frederick's

Chapel Market

Chapel Market

ANGEL

Noel Rd

The Island Queen

Olive

White Lion St

ANGEL

⊖ BUS

⊖ 🚲

Duncan Terrace

19,38,43,73,56,341

MAP

18

NW1

Adelaide Rd

BUS
31, N31

CHALK
FARM

Chal

N

Lemonia

The
Lansdowne

Cafe
Seventy
Nine

Regents Park Rd

22

23

ger Rd

21

Primrose Hill
Books

Gloucester Avenue

10 mins. walk

PRIMROSE HILL

Charlotte Square

Fitzroy Rd

Melrose
& Morgan

The
Queens

The Princess
of Wales

Primrose Hill Rd

L'Absinthe

24

25

26

Queens
No1

Princess Rd

The
Engineer

Towpath Camden Town

Regents canal

Regents Park Rd

Primrose Hill

BUS
274

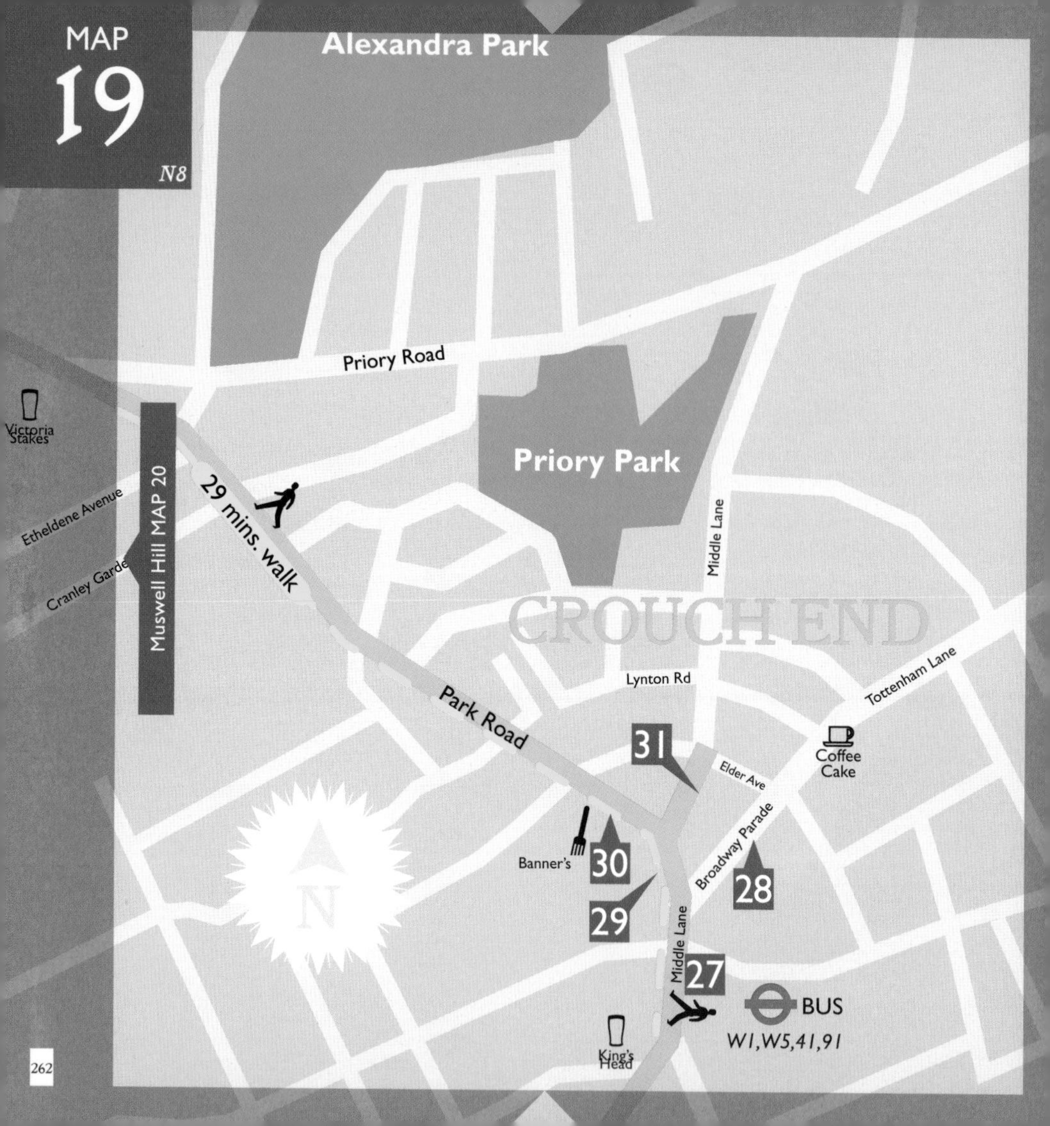

MAP
19
N8

Alexandra Park

Priory Road

Victoria
Stakes

Etheldene Avenue

Cranley Garde

Muswell Hill MAP 20

29 mins. walk

Priory Park

Middle Lane

CROUCH END

Park Road

Lynton Rd

Tottenham Lane

Coffee
Cake

31

Elder Ave

Banner's

30

Broadway Parade

29

28

Middle Lane

27

🚇 BUS
W1,W5,41,91

King's
Head

MAP

20

EAST
FINCHLEY

3 mins.

Bald
Faced
Stag

The
Alexandra

Queen's Ave

36

31

32

BUS
43,102,134,234,
N10

Princes Ave

Ave Mews

W Martyn

Clissold
Arms

Muswell Hill

37

Fortis Green Rd

Feast

£

Muswell Hill Broadway

Fortis Green Ave

Birchwood Ave

35 **34**

33

Victori
Stakes

Crouch End MAP 19

Etheldene

MUSWELL HILL

Cranley Gardens

Cranley

Muswell Hill Rd

Queens Wood

N

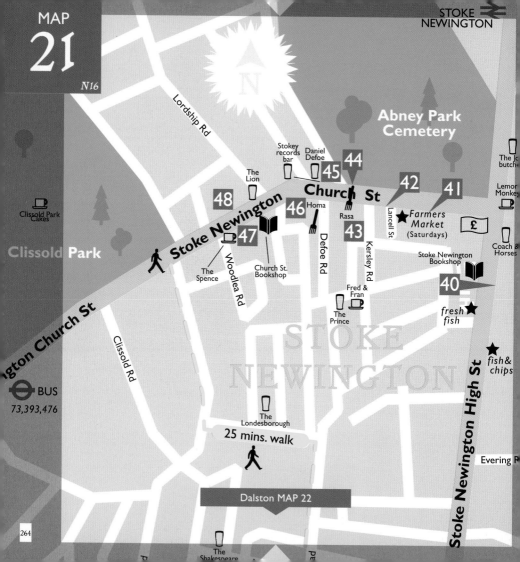

MAP
21
N16

STOKE
NEWINGTON

Lordship Rd

Abney Park
Cemetery

The Jo
butche

Stokey
records
bar

Daniel
Defoe

44

45

42

41

Lemor
Monkey

The
Lion

Church St

48

Homa

46

Rasa

Lancell St

Farmers
Market
(Saturdays)

£

Coach &
Horses

Clissold Park
Cakes

Stoke Newington

47

43

Kersley Rd

Stoke Newington
Bookshop

Clissold Park

The
Spence

Woodlea Rd

Church St.
Bookshop

Defoe Rd

40

Fred &
Fran

fresh
fish

STOKE

Clissold Rd

The Prince

NEWINGTON

fish &
chips

BUS
73,393,476

The
Londesborough

25 mins. walk

Stoke Newington High St

Evering R

Dalston MAP 22

The
Shakespeare

MAP
22

E8/N16

Albion Rd

Shakespeare Walk

Wordsworth

Stoke Newington MAP 21

54

Stoke Newin

Trattoria Sapori

Ruby Blue

55

London Print Club

☆

53

Miller's Ave

Moustache bar

Arcola Street

Barrets Grove

☆ Kristina records

Mangal Ocakbasi

Shackle

BUS 236

DALSTON

Bardens Boudoir

Newington Green

Somine Restaurant

Mildmay Rd

Boleyn Road

Dalston Superstore ★

⊖ **BUS**

67,76,149,243

Queen Margarets Grove

Rio Cinema ●

52

Alibi ★

Ridley Road Market

Ridley Rd

Ridley Road Market Bar

Vortex Jazz Bar ★

Bradbury St

Kingsland High St

Arcola Theatre

☆ Dalston Roofpark

51

Alma

King Henry's Walk

● ⊔ Cafe Oto

DALSTON KINGSLAND

RY

£

The Wellington

Balls Pond Rd

⊖ **BUS**

30,38,56,277

DALSTON JUNCTION ⊖

Dalston Lane

50

49

Ref.49 Storm In A Teacup
8 mins walk down Kingsland Rd.
at Middleton Rd.

Green Rd

265

THE MOROCCO STORE

Sainsbury's & Tesco stores kill small shops.
We don't want any more of them here
NEW CROSS FEDERATION

aurie Grove

South London foodies (as well as a vast number of tourists) have long delighted in Borough Market, though if you'd rather avoid the bustle, new upstart Maltby Street Market down the road in Bermondsey is quickly gaining popularity. Here, an eclectic collection of stall holders – from Monmouth Coffee to The Ham & Cheese Co – sell their wares from under a dotted network of railway arches. The enterprise reflects the area's independent, resourceful and creative spirit – one you'll find bubbling all over South London. Look to The Deptford Project for an ingenious community café housed in an old Tube carriage, or to the Young Vic in Waterloo for a characterful theatre that began life in a derelict butcher's shop and has grown into a leading London arts venue.

TROTTERS INDEPENDENT TRADING Co
NEW YORK - PARIS - PECKHAM

SE10 *Greenwich*

SE22 *East Dulwich*

SE14/SE15 *Peckham*

SE1 *Waterloo*

SE1 *Bermondsey*

SE1 *Borough*

SW4 *Clapham*

SOUTH

Royal Hill boasts a thread of high-quality food shops, which sell produce that is a million miles away from that found on the shelves of Tesco. **The Cheeseboard** sits a few doors along from Drings Butcher – both owned by Mike Jones, who has experience and passion for good quality food produce. The shop – open since 1985 – offers over 100 varieties of English and Continental cheeses and the knowledgeable staff are on-hand to offer their best cheesy advice. Freshly baked artisan bread is displayed above the cheese counters and the country-style baskets below are filled with traditional oatcakes and savoury biscuits. There's a good selection of chutneys, pickles and olives available and you can buy wine here too as well as a hand picked selection of pale ales and beers. *RL*

MAP 23 Ref. 5
The Cheeseboard
26 Royal Hill
Greenwich SE10 8RT
+44 (0)20 8305 0401
www.cheese-board.co.uk
Mon–Wed 9–5pm
Thu 9–1pm Fri 9–5.30pm
Sat 8.30–4.30pm

Cherry Picked is a unique designer boutique in Greenwich Market is very special indeed, Phyllis Taylor bought the shop over 5 years ago and has used her cultural background to bring a little slice of Ghana to London. Using fair-trade fabrics sourced from her parents' home town in Ghana, Phyllis has designed a capsule collection of women and children's clothing using classic 50s and 60s shapes. The 'Sika' label is based on simplicity and flattering feminine shapes and the clothing range is reasonably priced given its designer reputation. The Sika designs – which change seasonally – have been featured in Grazia, Vogue, East Living, You and the Daily Mirror – to name but a few. The combination of ethnic fabrics, retro shapes, made-to-measure designs (on request) and staff who truly care about the label, create an impressive, independent boutique worthy of a visit. *RL*

MAP 23 Ref. 1

Cherry Picked
5a Greenwich Market
Greenwich SE10 9HZ
+44 (0)20 8858 8158
www.sikadesigns.co.uk
Mon–Fri 12–6pm
Sat–Sun 12–6pm

Greenwich . *Fashion*

Drings Butchers has a 45-year history and over the past four years Mike Jones has successfully managed to maintain its excellent reputation. If you only shop in supermarkets and think you've tasted 'proper' meat before, think again – the sausages here are all made on the premise and contain a minimum of 97% free-range pork. All of the meat is free-range and the pork and poultry is sourced from a reputable farm in Suffolk. Emphasis is on well-reared, good quality meat. You can expect a personal touch at Drings too – staff know their regular customers by name and you can even call in advance to pre-order cuts of meat if you have a specific dish in mind. *RL*

MAP 23 Ref. 4

Drings Butchers
22 Royal Hill
Greenwich SE10 8RT
+44 (0)20 8858 4032
www.drings.co.uk
Mon–Wed 9–5pm
Thu 9–1pm Fri 9–5.30pm
Sat 8.30–4.30pm

The Fishmonger is quietly tucked away in a village-style area away from the main tourist throng. Not your usual fishmonger, this little fish shop offers a full selection of fresh, cooked and frozen fish, seafood, dressed crabs and tinned fish as well as gourmet accompaniments such as sauces, spices, sea salt, oils, vinegars, and fresh samphire. The fish is freshly sourced from a family-run business based on the Cornish coastline as well as Billingsgate Market. Sustainability is firmly in mind too – you certainly won't find bluefin tuna in this fishmonger. The fish is cut to order and staff can advise which are the best cuts available for sushi, should you like to try your hand at Japanese cuisine. *RL*

MAP 23 Ref. 6

The Fishmonger
Circus Street / rear of
26 Royal Hill
Greenwich SE10 8RT
+44 (0)7880 541485
www.thefishmongerltd.com
Tue–Fri 8.30–5pm
Sat 7.30–4.30pm

Greenwich . **Food**

271

Pickwick Papers & Fabrics

This is the type of shop that will make you want to instantly redecorate your house and be creative. With an inspiring collection of unique wallpaper designs, fabrics, bedding, blinds, curtains, carpets and paint – you'll be stocking up your basket faster than you can say 'changing rooms'! Renowned as one of London's finest interior design shops, **Pickwick Papers & Fabrics** have been in business since 1985 and even offer an interior design service for those needing professional advice. Whatever your need, big or small, staff at Pickwick are happy to help. *RL*

MAP 23 Ref. 2
Pickwick Papers & Fabrics
6 Nelson Road
Greenwich SE10 9JB
+44 (0)20 8858 1205
www.pickwickpapers.co.uk
Tue–Sat 9.30–5pm
Sun 11–3pm

Royal Teas is a rare gem in London: this cosy little café is the type of place where everyone knows your name if you're a regular – cheers! Of course you can remain incognito should that be your wish. The independent café boasts a predominately vegetarian menu that changes every other day. You can expect a tasty choice for breakfast, soups, salads, sandwiches, freshly-ground coffee and loose leaf and herbal teas. There's a reasonably-priced cream tea on the menu, as well as a dangerously tempting selection of cakes that are freshly made on the premise. As for the décor – brightly coloured exposed brick walls displaying local artwork, wooden floors and cosy little tables create a nice warm arty atmosphere. You can sit outside too, if the sun decides to shine. *RL*

MAP 23 Ref. 7

Royal Teas
76 Royal Hill
Greenwich SE10 8RT
+44 (0)20 8691 7240
www.royalteascafe.co.uk
Mon–Fri 9.30–5.30pm
Sun 10–6pm
Sun 10.30–6pm

Just a hop skip and a jump from Greenwich station, **Stitches & Daughters** provides a veritable treasure trove of homeware goods, gifts and classic designer clothing with a contemporary edge – just follow your nose. The shop houses a range of scented candles made by various companies, some relaxing, some rejuvenating and all impossible to put down without one last sniff. There's also a fabulous range of children's toys and irresistibly cute leather booties for babies as well as handmade cushions, carved wooden doorstoppers, unique gift wrap and pretty ribbons. This village-style shop is girly heaven, with its heady scents, pretty products and friendly staff. *RL*

MAP 23 Ref. 3
Stitches & Daughters
3 Greenwich South Street
Greenwich SE10 8NW
+44 (0)20 8305 1396
www.stitchesanddaughters.co.uk
Mon–Fri 10–5.30pm
Sat 10–5pm

Fairies & Floozies – one could be forgiven for thinking that this might be East Dulwich's first 'adult' shop. On the contrary, this is a chic little boutique tucked away down a quiet road next to the station, which sells an eclectic range of affordable designer clothing – with not a nipple tassel in sight. Leather belts, handmade jewellery, handbags and clothing from labels such as Religion, Max C, Yuki and T Style are displayed throughout the boudoir-style interior. Clothing and accessories are sourced by the owner who has 14 years' of solid fashion experience and the collection changes seasonally – giving us the perfect excuse to pop in on a regular basis. Also in tune with the local community, the shop arranges various events including 'styling nights' – you can't get more niche than that in East Dulwich. *RL*

MAP 24 Ref. 8

Fairies & Floozies
16 Melbourne Grove
East Dulwich SE22 8QZ
+44 (0)20 8299 3939
www.fairiesandfloozies.com
Mon–Fri 12–7pm
Sat 10–6.30pm
Sun 12.30–4.30pm

Fairies & Floozies

Mrs Robinson

In the heart of East Dulwich a colourful cave of gifts, vintage Danish furniture, clothing, kitchen- and homeware awaits. The ceiling is adorned with colour-pop silk shades that can be made to order depending on your colour preference and the shelves are positively brimming with contemporary products that would make a quirky and modern addition to any home. The furniture section features an eclectic range of vintage leather sofas, coffee tables and retro lamps and towards the back of the shop there's also an extensive collection of decorative mirrors. In the back of the shop there is a menswear boutique selling a range of casual designer clothing and labels such as Calvin Klein. It doesn't end there – across the road **Mrs Robinson** also has a dedicated boutique for ladies selling classic designs for smart women who like their clothing a little edgy. *RL*

MAP 24 Ref. 10

Mrs Robinson
153 Lordship Lane
East Dulwich SE22 8HX
+44 (0)20 8613 1970
www.mrsrobinsons.co.uk
Mon–Sat 10–5.30pm
Sun 12–5pm

Old Villa certainly has the last word in understated elegance, complete with rustic floorboards, original and ornate tiling and fragranced with the delicious scent of their range of candles and diffusers. Specialising in furniture and soft furnishings with a feel of faded grandeur, along with a selection of elegant glassware including carafes, bell jars and cake stands most of the collection is handmade and comes from France, Sweden and Belgium. Delicate handmade ceramics come in subtle colours complementing the neatly edited collection of nightwear and luxury casual pieces in gorgeous cashmere, silk, cotton and jersey in soft colours, all Old Villa's own collection. Large oxidised mirrors, table lamps, sideboards, day beds and side tables all inspired by antiques along with cosy blankets and throws complete the aesthetic of a stylish French country house. *PB*

MAP 24 Ref. 11
Old Villa
143 Lordship Lane
East Dulwich SE21 8HX
+44 (0)208 299 6966
www.artwords.co.uk
Tue–Sat 10– 6pm
Sun 11–5pm

Reminiscent of an old apothecary, a visit to **Roullier White** is an all together pleasant experience. Visualise walls lined with vintage wooden cabinets filled with products that are both attractive and functional. The fresh floral notes from exclusive scented candles waft through the shop whilst the informative staff are on-hand to provide friendly advice – they can even tell you which perfume is the perfect choice for you. This lifestyle boutique is a unique and refreshing addition to south London, it opened five years ago and has since attracted an abundance of press coverage. They sell an eclectic range of goods ranging from kitchenware, exclusive perfumes, men's toiletries, bathroom products, jewellery and garden products. The owner's great grandma was the inspiration behind the Mrs White's range: products inspired by her natural recipes, remedies, notions and potions. Beautifully packaged and environmentally friendly it's difficult not to buy the entire range. *RL*

MAP 24 Ref. 9
Roullier White
125 Lordship Lane
East Dulwich SE22 8HU
+44 (0)20 8693 5150
www.roullierwhite.com
Mon–Sat 10–6pm
Sun 11–5pm

Milk	Dark	White	Milk	Dark	Milk	Dark	white	Dark	Milk	Dark	white	Milk
GINGER	BERGAMOT	COCONUT	COFFEE	ORANGE	LAVENDER	5 SPICES	CARDAMOM	BASIL	CORIANDER	RASPBERRY	Matcha	Cumin
&	&	&	&	&	&	&	&	&	&	&		&
LIME	Cinnamon	VANILLA	ANISEED	CHILLI	LEMON	LEMONGRASS	NUTMEG	LEMON	GRAPEFRUIT	ROSEMARY	STRAWBERRY	MINT

The Melange Chocolates are pure Cocoa butter & Guaranteed free of NUTs, preservatives or additives. ONLY natural ingredients

Melange chocolate

With its pretty shop front and intoxicating aromas, **Melange chocolate** literally lures you in from the street. Of course, those in the know won't need much persuading: the boutique's unusual chocolates and indulgently thick, secret recipe hot chocolate are legendary in Peckham and beyond. For the uninitiated, bowls of sample chocs are filled with Melange's curious flavours such as ginger and lime, coriander and grapefruit or cumin and mint, while full-sized blocks are handsomely

wrapped and ready to take away. Self-taught chocolatier Isabelle Alaya does a remarkable job of making each inspired combination a delicate and delicious one, and also manages to turn out sensational fresh truffles and a heavenly rich chocolate cake. The Frenchwoman is happy to pass on her enviable knowledge too, and she regularly holds in-store tastings and workshops. ZA

MAP 26 Ref. 18

Melange chocolate
184 Bellenden Road
Peckham SE15 4BW
+44 (0)7722 650 711
www.themelange.com
Tue–Fri 12–7pm
Sat–Sun 10–6pm

Peckham . Café

Free truffle with any drink*

Keeping good company among a small enclave of independent shops on Bellenden Road, **Otherwise** provides Peckham locals with a taste of couture. The boutique is headed up by Christopher Morris – a Central St Martin's graduate with more than 40 years experience in fashion design – and draws on the wider talents of his creative family. The in-store collection showcases Morris's alternative design vision, with plenty of deconstruction, recycled materials and a bold use of colour worked into distinctive apparel.

It's a style that's particularly popular with Peckham's more arty residents, though affordable price tags mean it won't cost a bomb to stand out from the crowd. If you're after something truly one-off, Morris also works to commission and offers some of the area's finest made-to-measure and alteration services, weaving in his own magic along the way. ZA

MAP 26 Ref. 20

Otherwise
141 Bellenden Road
Peckham SE15 4DH
+44 (0)20 8635 8044
www.otherwisewear.com
Mon–Sat 10–6.30pm
Sun 11–3pm

-15%

Discount *

South Londoners with a penchant for retro would do well to skip a trip to the east end and head instead to **Threads**, this neighbourhood vintage boutique where Peckham local Tara Postma offers a fine, handpicked selection of women's, men's and children's apparel. The choice is broad, with the front of the store dedicated to affordable garb including bargain frocks from the '60s and '70s as well as an excellent range of men's blazers. Rare designer finds and more delicate vintage pieces can be found at the back and, if you're in luck, you might spot a velvet Vivienne Westwood mini skirt for as little as £60 or a vintage Burberry trench for just £80. A brief but appealing collection of hats, shoes and accessories also feature. ZA

MAP 26 Ref. 19

Threads
186 Bellenden Road
Peckham SE15 4BW
+44 (0)7741599407
www.vintagethreadspeckham.
wordpress.com
Tues–Wed 11–6pm
Thu–Sat 11–7pm
Sun 11–4pm

Peckham . *Fashion*

Birksen is not just a flower shop; it is more of a lifestyle statement. As Birksen's philosophy says, "flowers make us happy". Here you won't just find the most beautiful and fresh tulips, peonies, dahlias or roses but also every single accessory that will frame your preferred arrangement in the best way as well as seeds, gardening equipment and an array of bits and pieces that will help you create a mini paradise on earth, even that special setting that you are after. Birksen also specialises in providing all flower arrangements for any kind of event: from weddings, to parties and corporate events, even magazine shoots. Staff are very friendly and will help you put together a nice bouquet if you want to win over that grumpy neighbour or impress the girl of your dreams; you don't even have to release your inner charmer. Birksen's flowers will do the work. *DG*

MAP 25 Ref. 13
Birksen
40 Old Town
Clapham SW4 0LB
+44 (0)20 7622 6466
www.birksen.co.uk
Mon–Fri 8.30–5.30pm
Sat 10–5pm
Sun 10.30–4pm

JZD is one of those boutiques that even if you don't intend on buying anything, you are sure not to leave empty-handed. Situated in Clapham's quaint old Town, it combines cool fashion and a bit of history. And who doesn't find that a bit tempting? Occupying a three-storey townhouse, which also happens to be Clapham's oldest building, JZD is filled with some of the coolest womenswear brands, like danish 'By Malene Birger', spanish 'Hoss Intropia', Trevor Bolongaro, affordable jewellery as well as cool menswear names, like Superdry and Gio Goi, makers of quirky t-shirts, or in other words 'cool things to go in your wardrobe and stay there for years'. It may be just over ten years old, but it has still got the buzz, as owners Raj Wilkinson and his wife Sam, a former Selfridges buyer, still scout the world for the coolest and funkiest offerings. One thing is for sure: you will come again, and again, and again. *DG*

MAP 25 Ref. 14
JZD
45 Old Town
Clapham SW4 0JL
www.jzdstyle.co.uk
+44 (0)20 7720 8050
Mon–Wed 10–6pm
Thu–Fri 10–7pm
Sat 10-6:30pm
Sun 12-6pm

Les Sardines

Italian Leopoldina Haynes used to work at one of London's famous auction houses as a watches specialist, until she decided to give it all up to pursue her passion for interiors. Just a year old, **Les Sardines** specialises in French and Swedish antiques (for example, an 18th c French armoire or a 19th c chest of drawers) which Leopoldina searches out around the world using her keen eye, but also those small bits and pieces that make a difference; from vintage mugs and jugs, lavender pouches and linen cushion covers to Italian soaps, even cute, little notebooks. The best thing about the shop: its affordability factor (prices start at £5) and friendly vibe. As she says, 'Antiques can be off-putting but I wanted to create a place where anybody can buy anything, a place that makes you want to go away with something'. DG

MAP 25 Ref. 17
Les Sardines
63 Abbeville Road
Clapham SW4 9JW
+44 (0)20 8675 3900
www.lessardines.co.uk
Tue–Sat 10–6pm
Sun 12–4pm

Home . Clapham

A 40-year-old family business, now owned and run by Garry Moen, son of founder Maurice, **M. Moen & Sons** is one of Clapham's, if not London's, great butchers and delicatessen shops. For a start, the interior will blow you away: restored to its former Victorian glory with the help of a National Lottery grant, this place is filled with every kind of meat imaginable and of the highest quality: free-range or organic beef, own-made sausages, venison, poultry and game. And not just that, the shop also has a special section on cheeses and cold cuts, like Parma and Serrano ham as well as an amazing deli counter, where you can find pickles, mustards, chutneys and jams. Did we mention the weekly confit, pate and cassoulet deliveries from France? Or even the daily fruit and mushroom offerings from local independent farmers? M. Moen& Sons is not just a gourmet shop, but rather a precious address in your notebook if good quality nutrition is high on your agenda. DG

MAP 25 Ref. 15
M. Moen & Sons
24 The Pavement
Clapham SW4 0JA
+44 (0)20 7622 1624
www.moen.co.uk
Mon–Fri 8.30–6.30pm
Sat 8.30-5pm

Clapham. **Food**

Let's say you are after an Achille Castiglioni Arco 1962 lamp, or an Alvar Aalto vase, even a Verner Panton Tivoli dining chair. Well, **Places & Spaces** is definitely your place. A must shop for hardcore design aficionados, this shop plays host to a pretty fine collection of some of the most iconic pieces of 20th century design (anything from furniture to accessories and lighting). But its forte is not just cult design classics: Places & Spaces also sources and stocks modern favourites such as pieces by Droog or Ronan and Erwan Bouroullec to name just a few, positioning itself as the ultimate space for exploring design. Its trusted team will also provide help, should you decide to put all these old and modern classics under one roof and even create a unique look for your office or apartment. Should you want to delve more into the world of design, check out the frequent activities it organises, especially, the interesting design exhibitions it curates all around London. DG

MAP 25 Ref. 12

Places and Spaces
30 Old Town
Clapham SW4 OLB
+44 (0)20 7498 0998
www.placesandspaces.com
Tue–Sat 10–5.45pm
Sun 12 – 4pm

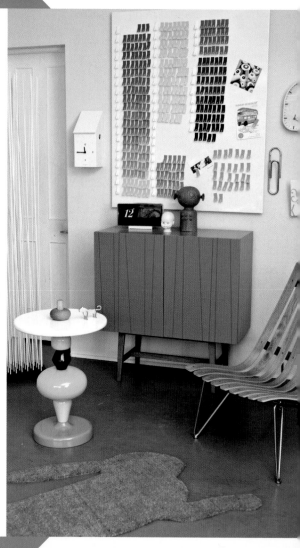

Everyone is welcome to drop in and stich (or just have a slice of cake) at this homely sewing café. An in-house haberdashery supplies everything you need to get cracking on that project – from buttons to fabrics and patterns galore – while workstations and a communal table house Janome sewing machines, scissors and irons. Crafty types are welcome to drop by for £5 an hour (a price which includes free tea) or sign up for specific workshops. Beginners can get a sewing taster with classes such as 'intro to sewing' or 'men's survival sewing', while dab hands can book into the 'ultimate shift dress' or 'pussy bow blouse'. Knitting and gift-making workshops also feature. If you're not handy with a needle, but love homemade craft, cute gifts (such as fabric-backed pocket mirrors) serve as yet another reason to give **Sew Over It** a visit. ZA

MAP 25 Ref. 16

Sew Over It
78 Landor Road
Clapham SW9 9PH
+44 (0)20 7326 0376
www.sewoverit.co.uk
Mon closed
Tues–Fri 1–6pm
Sat 10–6pm
Sun 12–5pm

Clapham . **Crafts**

287

Bermondsey Street is fast cementing itself as a go-to shopping destination and it's largely thanks to independent boutiques like **Bermondsey 167**. Opened in 2007 by Michael McGrath and Allessandro Palhares – a pair whose collective CV lists design and buying roles with Gieves & Hawkes, Burberry and Prada – the eclectic store has become a favourite with style-conscious men as well as interior designers looking for unique furnishings. The store's specially designed and commissioned homeware celebrates natural materials, and you might spot fabulous bookends made from reclaimed wood or a lamp crafted from coconut leaf. For men, McGrath's own label, M2CG, offers a desirable range of quality shirts, silk ties and leather belts, while a good range of cufflinks also features. Elsewhere, you'll find a beautifully curated mix of pretty gifts, arty books and handcrafted, semi-precious jewellery. *ZA*

MAP 27 Ref. 27

Bermondsey 167
167 Bermondsey street
Bermondsey SE1 3UW
+44 (0)20 7407 3137
www.bermondsey167.com
Tues–Fri 11–7pm
Thu 8pm
Sat 10–7pm
Sun 12–6pm

-10%

Discount on selected menswear and jewellery*

Named after the French word for 'wine cellar', **Cave** sells the quality things in life and is ideal for a little something to bring to a dinner party. They offer expert advice, proudly declaring, "We love to help people choose". A gap in the local market for designer fresh cut flowers, specially chosen wines and exquisite artisan chocolates ethically sourced presented itself and thus Cave was born. With a homely pared down English environment the shop smells delicious with flowers and autumn leaves.

All the wine is produced on a small scale and is bio-dynamic and organic and the shop packaging is 100% recycled and untreated, being good for the planet as well as stylish. Their products are very well thought out and edited so that every purchasing decision is a good one, "we know the market well round here, we have an aesthetic response to our community". *PB*

MAP 27 Ref. 28

Cave
210 Bermondsey Street
Bermondsey SE1 3TQ
+44 (0)20 0011 4701
www.cavelondon.com
Mon–Sat 10–8pm

With a tagline "All beautiful things made with love" this community embracing shop is about just that. All the products you will find here come from either locals or friends of the owner making **Bermondsey Fayre** a very apt name. Everything is ethically sourced, fair trade and handmade from paintings to clothes to chutney, giving the shop an arts and crafts feel. Regular workshops teaching an assortment of fun classes including making fancy knickers, sock monkeys, floral brooches and even your own beauty products keeps the theme of the shop eclectic and fun creating a real community spirit, "We think that rather than just being a shop it's a good opportunity to offer more than that". A great place to buy something both pleasing and handy is summed up in a photograph from a local photographer stating "Have nothing in your home that you do not know to be useful, or believe to be beautiful". PB

MAP 27 Ref. 29

Bermondsey Fayre
212 Bermondsey Street
Bermondsey SE1 3TQ
+44 (0)20 7403 2133
www.bermondseyfayre.co.uk
Wed–Sat 11.30–7pm

A curious mix of council estates, high-end residential properties and converted warehouses, Bermondsey is the ideal spot for an edgy shop like the **Cockfighter of Bermondsey**. This playful and flirty boutique stocks a fashionable range of eye-catching men and woman's clothing from humorously camp skull and cross bone printed Y-fronts and frilly knickers to a selection of fifties-style bowling shirts and dresses. Branded under the Cockfighter and Cock & Magpie labels you'll find hats, belts, bags and jewellery alongside a range of branded and logo-ed T-shirts (with slogans such as 'honk if you had it last night'), denim and casual wear emblazoned with the distinctive Cockfighter logo. With a tight London theme including handmade cards which celebrate London scenes the clothes are named after London spots Shoreditch, Hackney and, of course, Bermondsey. *PB*

MAP 27 Ref. 26

Cockfighter of Bermondsey
96 Bermondsey Street
Bermondsey SE1 3UB
+44 (0)20 7357 6482
www.cockandmadpie.com
Tue by appointment
Wed & Sat 10–6pm
Thu–Fri 11–7pm
Sun 11–5pm

Cockfighter of Bermondsey

London Glassblowing Workshop

could easily be mistaken as just an upmarket showroom displaying glassware is in fact one of the most innovative galleries around. With a gallery space upfront the back is a fully functioning workshop where visitors can bring a cup of coffee, pull up a chair and watch the process in action. Trained artisans in various stages of the procedure create stunning pieces in front of your eyes. An informal environment that bridges the gap between artist and viewer where they are happy to answer any questions you may have. Regular glassblowing classes are held where you can learn the process first hand along with evening events and exhibitions. Raging furnaces known as 'reheating chambers' or to the experts, 'Glory Holes' keep the room toasty warm so it's easy to get comfortable and while a way an afternoon watching molten glass transform into the exquisite pieces they have on display. *PB*

MAP 27 Ref. 24

London Glassblowing Workshop
62–66 Bermondsey Street
Bermondsey SE1 3UD
+44 (0)20 7403 2800
www.londonglassblowing.co.uk
Mon–Sat 10–5pm

If you're ever lost on Tower Bridge Road, you'd do well to find the lovely **Lost and Found**. The shop stars a farrago of furniture supplied by a handful of vintage experts and covers rustic cabinets, stylish mid-twentieth century finds and alternative furnishings such as old gym boxes and school benches. The store also stocks gorgeous lighting by Madeleine Boulesteix who makes use of a medley of collected objects to make pretty chandeliers. Owner and textile designer Becky Oldfield has a particular penchant for all things British and does a sterling job of sourcing salvaged items from old transport signage to antique maps. She also presents her own textile pieces, which rework vintage textiles (old flags, fabrics and the like) with new materials for a contemporary homage to British heritage. ZA

MAP 27 Ref. 30

Lost and Found
77 Tower bridge road
Bermondsey SE1 4TW
+44 (0)7958324 038
www.lostandfounddesign.co.uk
Sat 11–5pm

Bermondsey . **Home**

-15%

Discount*

What makes this women's wear store **Pussy Willow** special is that everything you see can be made to your specific requirements and taste. Not only can they make pieces to fit you perfectly but you can request changes in both colours and fabric using only the best from Britain and France additionally lining all the garments with silk. They create a capsule collection of stylish pieces alongside stunningly glamorous full length dresses fit for the Oscars. With an atelier in the back all the garments are designed and produced onsite just like the proper couture houses of old. As and when new collections are designed, customers are invited along to see the process and inspiration behind the pieces creating a very personal experience, far from what you would find on the high street. *PB*

MAP 27 Ref. 25
Pussy Willow Coutoure
90 Bermondsey street
Bermondsey SE1 3UB
+44 (0)207 407 3024
www.pwillow.com
Tues–Fri 10.30–7pm
Sat 11–6pm
Sun 12–4pm

Who said that moving had to be a pain? **The Rocketvan Boxshop** provides a full removal and delivery service and even makes buying boxes and packaging material that little bit more fun. A bit like being in a giant cardboard box, the interior of the shop is comprised of cardboard, varnished MDF and pegboard, traditionally used in old hardware stores. They have a straightforward system of choosing boxes that range in dimensions and material, either plastic or cardboard and in every size from extra-small to extra-large and everything you might need from room contents labels to bubble wrap, brown tape and string. They even have some cleverly picked out things like cardboard birdhouses, welcome mats, tea-lights and decorative wall prints to furnish a room, making it a little bit more homely. A quirky approach to branding, you wouldn't find space invaders on the wall of your local DHL would you? *PB*

MAP 27 Ref. 23

The Rocketvan Boxshop
229–231 Union Street
Borough SE1 3TQ
+44 (0)20 7401 3928
www.rocketvan.co.uk
Mon–Sat 8–6pm

Well you can't miss it, the amusing yet worrying quote by George W Bush hanging from the window makes sure of that. Primarily a theatre bookshop they also have many books on politics, philosophy and poetry, everything from Arthur Miller to Shakespeare, alongside Samuel Beckett and books on fascism. With a little theatre in the back complete with velveteen chairs, the owners were keen to have a place to put on their own plays and the shop was just a happy addition. They invite other companies to perform just as long as they meet their obscure criteria. The enterprise is not about commerce but really just about a love for theatre. With window displays less about books and more about provocation, **The Calder Bookshop** certainly makes its presence felt. *PB*

MAP 27 Ref. 22
The Calder Bookshop & Theatre
51 The Cut
Waterloo SE1 8LF
+44 (0)20 7620 2900
www.calderbookshop.com/
Mon–Sat 10–5pm

It's not hard to fathom that in these fashionable times knitting will be right up there with fixed wheel bikes and warehouse raves as the latest thing considered the height of cool. Established by Craig who started knitting when he was seven, his first projects being clothes for his action men and Gerard who was confined to his couch with a back problem and needed something to do other than eat cake and watch telly, **I Knit** evolved from a community group with a shared love of knitting over a pint

of beer. Offering weekly classes for beginners and fun social get-togethers with champagne (they have a liquor licence) and croissants for those with more experience to swap tips. With the largest selection of knitting books and magazines in London and shelves packed with different varieties of wool, I Knit stock everything on the list for the beginner to the advanced. *PB*

MAP 27 Ref. 21

I Knit
106 Lower Marsh
Waterloo SE1 7AB
+44 (0)20 7261 1338
www.iknit.org.uk
Mon 11–6pm
Tue–Thu 11–9pm
Fri–Sat 11–6pm

Waterloo . *Crafts*

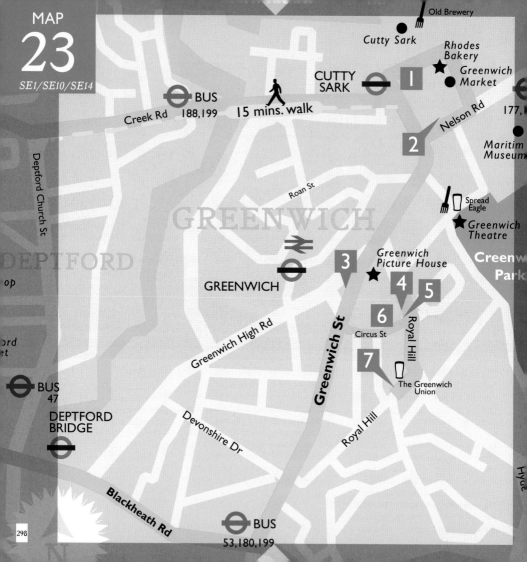

MAP

23

SE1/SE10/SE14

Old Brewery

Cutty Sark

Rhodes Bakery

★ *Greenwich Market*

CUTTY SARK ⊖ **1**

BUS 188,199

Creek Rd

🚶 **15 mins. walk**

Nelson Rd

177,

2

Maritim Museum

Deptford Church St

Roan St

GREENWICH

DEPTFORD

Spread Eagle

★ *Greenwich Theatre*

🚆

⊖ **3** ★ *Greenwich Picture House*

Greenwi Park

GREENWICH

4

5

6 Circus St

Royal Hill

Greenwich High Rd

Greenwich St

7

The Greenwich Union

⊖ BUS 47

DEPTFORD BRIDGE ⊖

Devonshire Dr

Royal Hill

Hyde

Blackheath Rd

⊖ BUS 53,180,199

N

MAP
24
SE22

EAST
DULWICH

BUS
40,176,185,484

Grove Vale

Goose Green

East Dulwic

Scooped

Ice cream

8

N

Deli

9 mins. walk

Cheese

Crawthew Grove

Crystal Palace Rd

East Dulwich Grove

BUS
37

Melbourne Grove

EAST DULWICH

Ashbourne Grove

£

BUS
40,176,185

Nuffield Rd

New Cross Rd

Blue
Mountain

Lordship Lane

9

10

11

Blackwater St

Bawdale Rd

LaChandalier

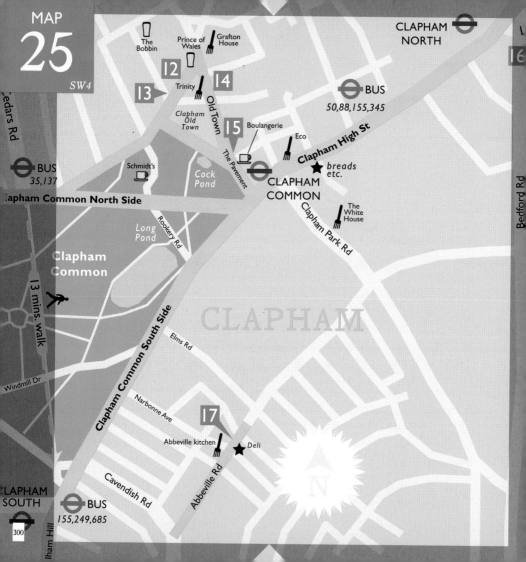

MAP
25

SW4

The Bobbin

Prince of Wales

Grafton House

12

13 Trinity

14

Old Town

Clapham Old Town

15 Boulangerie

CLAPHAM NORTH

BUS
50,88,155,345

Eco

Clapham High St

breads etc.

CLAPHAM COMMON

Schmidt's

Cedars Rd

BUS
35,137

Clapham Common North Side

Cock Pond

The Pavement

The White House

Clapham Park Rd

Bedford Rd

Long Pond

Rookery Rd

Clapham Common

13 mins. walk

Windmill Dr

Clapham Common South Side

Elms Rd

CLAPHAM

Narbonne Ave

17

Abbeville kitchen

Deli

Abbeville Rd

Cavendish Rd

CLAPHAM SOUTH

BUS
155,249,685

Ilham Hill

300

16

N

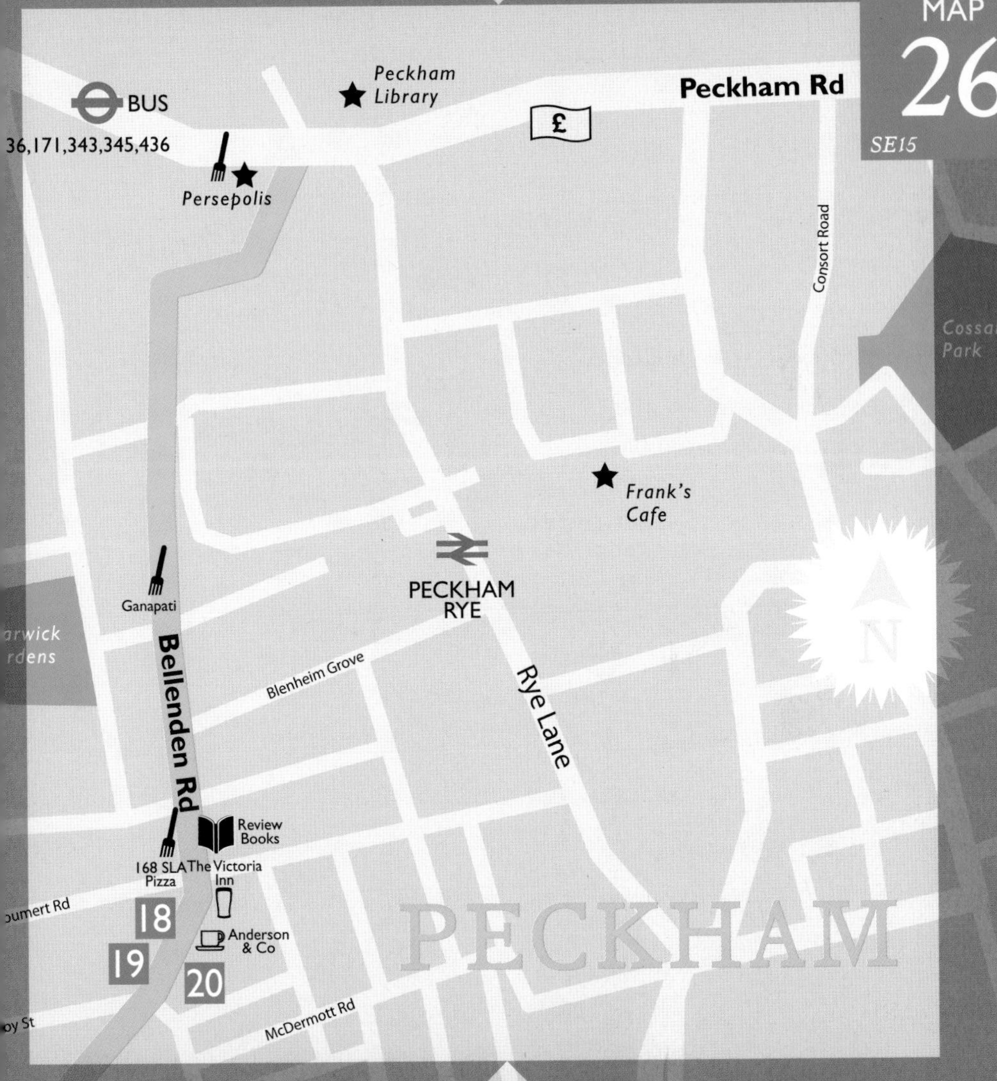

MAP

26

SE15

Peckham **Rd**

⊖ BUS

36,171,343,345,436

★ Peckham Library

£

Consort Road

Cossall Park

🍴
★ Persepolis

★ Frank's Cafe

⇄
PECKHAM RYE

🍴
Ganapati

Bellenden Rd

Blenheim Grove

Rye Lane

arwick rdens

📖 Review Books

🍴
168 SLA The Victoria Inn
Pizza 🍺

oumert Rd

18

19

☕ Anderson & Co

20

McDermott Rd

oy St

PECKHAM

MAP
27
SE1

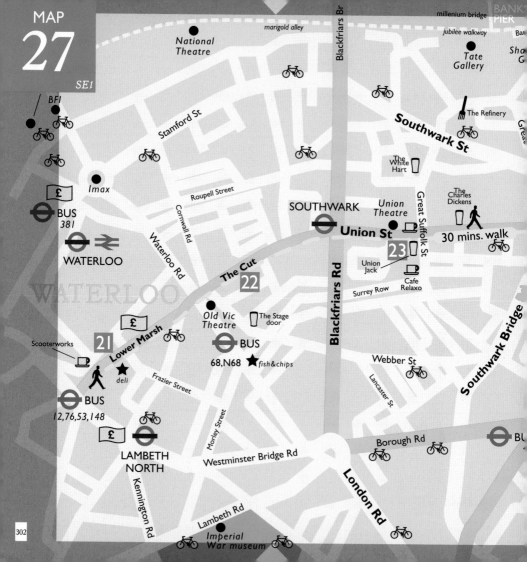

National Theatre

marigold alley

Blackfriars Br

millenium bridge

BANKS
PIER

jubilee walkway

Ba

Tate Gallery

Sha
G

The Refinery

Southwark St

Gre

BFI

Stamford St

Imax

Roupell Street

The White Hart

The Charles Dickens

£

BUS
381

Cornwall Rd

SOUTHWARK

Union Theatre

Great Suffolk St

30 mins. walk

WATERLOO

Waterloo Rd

Union St

23

WATERLOO

The Cut

22

Union Jack

Cafe Relaxo

Surrey Row

Scooterworks

£

Lower Marsh

21

Old Vic Theatre

The Stage door

BUS
68,N68

fish&chips

Blackfriars Rd

deli

Frazier Street

Webber St

Lancaster St

Southwark Bridge

BUS
12,76,53,148

Morley Street

£

LAMBETH
NORTH

Kennington Rd

Westminster Bridge Rd

Borough Rd

BU

London Rd

Lambeth Rd

Imperial War museum

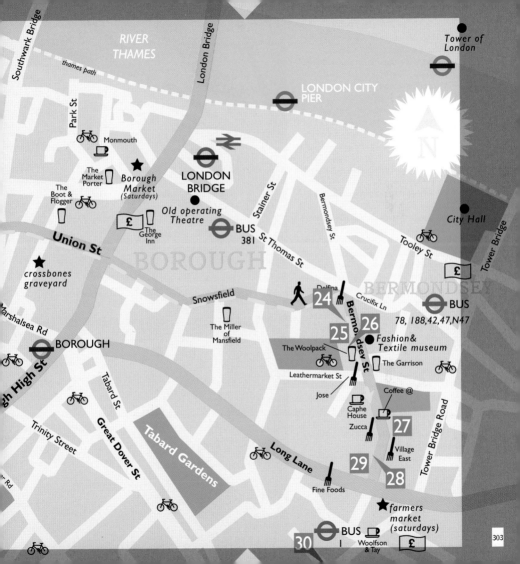

RIVER THAMES

Southwark Bridge

thames path

London Bridge

LONDON CITY PIER

Tower of London

Park St

Monmouth

The Market Porter

★ Borough Market (Saturdays)

LONDON BRIDGE

The Boot & Flogger

£

The George Inn

Old operating Theatre

BUS 381

Stainer St

Bermondsey St

City Hall

Tooley St

£

Tower Bridge

Union St

BOROUGH

★ crossbones graveyard

St Thomas St

BERMONDSEY

Marshalsea Rd

Snowsfield

The Miller of Mansfield

24

Dolfina

Crucifix Ln

BUS 78, 188,42,47,N47

25

26

Bermondsey St

Fashion & Textile museum

BOROUGH

The Woolpack

Leathermarket St

Jose

The Garrison

Tabard St

Great Dover St

Trinity Street

Tabard Gardens

Long Lane

Caphe House

Zucca

Coffee @

27

Village East

29

28

Tower Bridge Road

Fine Foods

★ farmers market (saturdays)

30

BUS

Woolfson & Tay

£

303

Perhaps there could not be a more difficult time to produce the 3rd Independent London Store Guide! Probably… possibly, but the individual independent shop is a glorious personal stamp of your own personality and spirit on life itself.

In this confusing and perilous sea, there are two elements; the shopkeeper and the shopper. Does the shopper delight at entering your shop? Are you the kind of person that is nice and friendly to the customers?

When I was a child my mother took me into Watson Prickards in Liverpool. Mr Cockeram senior was always there, as you entered, by the stairs with a glorious smile and a welcome; by name too. I can see him now. It was a superb shop –pricey, but people liked to go in. Of course you've also got to sell your stock this just means having what the customer wants or needs.

Here in Notting Hill we are having a fearsome battle to save the famous Portobello Antiques market from the international clone multiples. You know the kind of stores. You see them in every big city. Luckily we have reputable knowledgeable individuals who make the market so fascinating, Henry Gregory, Jeff Knowles and Barry Trice are just some of them. They'll tell you the pleasure of being master of your own destiny!

Next edition we'll explain all about rents, Local Authority Support etc!! It's no easy ride.

John Scott
Founder & Project Leader
Notting Hill Gate Improvement Group

Index *according to shop category*

★ = OFFERS

Continued overleaf

— • —

Acknowledgements and thank you's

REVIEWERS
Zena Alkayat
Penny Blood
Dimi Gaidatzi
Rebecca Lori
Fiona Mcdonald
Moritz Steiger
Tanis Taylor
Geraldine Turvey

DESIGN
Adrian Philpott / PHILPOTT Design Ltd.
www.PHILPOTTdesign.com

PHOTOGRAPHY
Moritz Steiger and Effie Fotaki
Copyright © 2012 Moritz Steiger and Effie Fotaki.
All rights reserved.

ILLUSTRATION (BACK COVER)
Roja Kerr

Many thanks to all the shops who gave their support in the making of this book and to all those sending their shop tips and for the direct support of whom we would like to thank by name, David McHugh and John Scott, without whose help this book would not have been possible.

This book is our small contribution to supporting the 260 independent shops we feature and we hope, support the local high streets and markets for the greater benefit of local communities. Keep your suggestions coming in. We hope you like it..

Effie and Moritz
guide@independentlondon.com
www.independentlondon.com

Revised third edition. Published by **MONSTERMEDIA**.
Copyright © 2012 Moritz Steiger and Effie Fotaki.
All rights reserved.